What Won't BREAK

A POETRY COLLECTION

Prince Harrison, Jr., CC Miller, & Ashley Wooten

Published by CC Miller, LLC

Copyright ©2022

Published by CC Miller, LLC

ISBN 979-8-218-06876-9

Printed in the United States of America.

All Rights Reserved.

thoughts and feelings toward you.

Warmest Regards,

Prince Harrison, Jr.   CC Miller   Ashley Wooten

Preface

The poetry in this anthology is the result of a mutual respect for the verbal prowess and genuine love of poetry and friendship shared among the authors and the community we love. It is real and raw and delivered with as much fervor on stage as written within these pages. We are thrilled that you are taking the time to read them. They are our babies and we're proud parents of this project. It is our desire that you will be proud of them, too.

One of Aesop's Fables, the Oak and the Reeds inspired the title for this anthology. There is a wisdom in knowing when yielding is the right and best course to take. There is a peace that comes with the freedom of knowing what cannot be taken or lost. There is elation in finding that what might have been perceived as broken was merely the growth and change to be expected for a masterful work to take its beautiful form. **What Won't BREAK** draws from stories of humble triumph to present our take on culture, experiences and people who have been formidable against the storms because of that humility and insightfulness.

Our deepest gratitude is reserved for our Father, and a large measure for our friends and family who love us enough to read our passions compassionately, insightfully, and not lose sight of us in the winds.

Ashley would like to dedicate this collection to her muses, her family, and her friends: "To our Heavenly Father, and to herself, I love you all so much. Thank you so much for keeping me strong. Because of your love, I won't break." Prince would like to dedicate this book "to my family & friends, thank y'all for the continuous support & love! I also want to thank the girl that broke my heart, because of that situation I was able to turn the pain into poetry for other people to read & enjoy. So, Bubsy, thank you. At the end of the day, sticks & stones may hurt my bones, but nothing in this world will break my spirit." As for CC, you all already know my

Contents

Groundbreaking — 13

Breakdown — 15

Outbreak — 16

Backbreaking — 17

Duplex I: Breakout — 18

Duplex II: Hurt Me — 20

The Jitters — 22

Stomach Knots — 24

Déjà Vu — 25

Can't Breathe — 26

The Feels — 28

Anxious Soul — 30

Take It Away — 32

What Won't Break II — 34

Built to Break — 36

Fatigue	38
Polish and Shelve	40
The Boring	41
We	43
Small, Low	47
When They Go/Rubber Boots	50
Confidence	51
Peace	52
In Dreaming Color…a Compilation	53
One for the Team	56
Sweet Life (Time's Past Pictured)	57
You're the "-EST"	59
Encounter	63
At All Costs	65
Creation Space	67
Breakfast	69

Break Away	70
Duplex III: Bleed in Emotion	72
Yesterday Night	74
Some People	77
Never Forget	78
Princykins	80
Let Me Heal	82
Forget-Me-Nots	84
Loud and Clear	86
It Fell	88
Spirited	91
Fruitage	92
Divinely Architectural	93
In the Days That Follow	95
Wish You…Well,	98
OMW (On My Way)	99

The School of Scarred Hearts   102

Meek Matter   103

Thumbs Up   104

Untouchables   106

What You Need (Short and Sweet)   110

Breaking News   112

Brake   114

What Won't Break I   115

Duplex IV: Fill That Void   116

Duplex V: Break Me   118

Duplex VI: Building   120

Loss & Leaving   122

Apologies   124

Caring Too Much   125

Scars On My Aorta II   126

Artist   128

Go 129

Can't Break Me 130

Forward 133

Yours, Wholly 134

Absence 135

The Best Thing About a Breakup 138

I Would Like to Love 144

We Were Pretending 145

What Mattered 148

Railroaded 151

Of Willows, Reeds, and Dandelions 154

See You (Meditation on Job 14:14,15 and John 5:28,29) 157

2015 161

Life lesson #6 165

AOA (Alive on Arrival) 166

Quiet Storm 169

RIP-Psalms 4 172

'A Note on Love.' Inspired by the Homie of all Homies 174

Unbreakable 177

Daybreak 179

Duplex VII: Breaking Windows 180

Duplex VIII: Breakthrough 182

Duplex VIIII: Wildfire 184

Duplex X: September 2027 186

Her Perspective 188

His Perspective 190

Like I Used to Before 192

Liar 195

Jawbreaker 197

Broken Bubsy 198

Storyteller	207
In Flight	209
Amalgamated	210
Sound Barrier	211
I Wasn't	213
Cutting Remarks	214
Cracks in the Sidewalk	216
Gravel and Glass	217
Gaslight	218
Breaking point	220
Death Defying	224
Edges	225
Omelet	227
Raggedy Blue Things	230
Breaks	232
Escaped Convict	234

And It Rains   236

Stumbling   237

How to Puzzle Out a Puzzle   239

Purpose   242

"Love Lettered"   243

Executive Decision   250

Inside Story   251

Utter Abundance (Heart Speak)   252

Puzzled   256

BOUND

Groundbreaking

Prince Harrison, Jr.

Tectonic Plates shake my neurons like

an 8.0 magnitude earthquake

Seismic waves take my breath away

like a punch to the esophagus

Blue flames surround the ring of fire

The focus vibrates &

splits the ground at an angle

Landslides leap for joy like the deer

A violent event that leaves

no prisoners behind

The chains of earth are broken

The ground opens up and

consumes human flesh like sugar

The faults create chaos & confusion

Wave fronts slam across the border

And the walls of earth crumble

to pieces like Jericho

An earth quaking in fear

A mother shaking in tears

A world breaking more every year

Breakdown

Prince Harrison, Jr.

I break down

Cry my eyes out

Suffer in silence

Silence the pain

My pen writes but

My neurons stop working

Ink oozes down the table

Like a colossal squid

And I freeze

like a popsicle

Outbreak

Prince Harrison, Jr.

Sneeze into the breeze

Cough inside a loft

Particles spread faster than a wildfire

Bacteria move faster than an airplane

Stuffy nose

Catching a cold

Billions sick

The clock ticks

Sin is a pandemic

Backbreaking

Prince Harrison, Jr.

I carry her

She doesn't carry me

This dependency is backbreaking

I think about her every hour of the day

I simply can't shake this feeling

I try my hardest to stop thinking about her

But I can't

I can't carry the weight of loneliness

I can't carry the anvil of sadness

I can't carry the dumbbell of pain

My spine snaps & my vertebrae cracks

Another tragic case

Of a broken sacroiliac

Duplex I: Breakout

Prince Harrison, Jr.

A bomber flies over my head
Men of flesh left me for dead

The flesh of men lies down on the ground
Women & children tremble in fear

Fear swallows the children, women cry tears
A glass mirror shines in the distance

A diamond ring shines in the distance
A man falls in love with a woman

A man becomes infatuated with a woman
He shoots for the stars, but misses the target

An archer closes his eyes and misses the target
A runaway bride

A runaway groom

Love at first sight

Lies at first sight

A bomber flies over my head

Duplex II: Hurt Me

Prince Harrison, Jr.

She hurt me again & I feel weak

Her pretty face lies in a pool of deceit

Pretty faces always have deceit to hide

I took a trip to Bat City

I almost didn't make it back from Bat City

She checked on me everyday

She doesn't check on me anymore

I gave her my secrets & promised my love

She took my secrets & ripped them with hate

She asks: When will you learn your lesson?

I ask myself: When will I learn from my mistakes?

I poured her in a beaker, and called her sugar

She doused me in gasoline and called me Sugar

They told me she was a danger, and I gave chase

I gave chase to danger, I'm a broken blue vase

She hurt me again & I feel weak

The Jitters

Prince Harrison, Jr.

I feel like a 2-liter bottle of Sprite

A molecule trapped in giant plastic

My arms feel weak

My brain is doing a thousand jumping jacks

My mind is spinning like a merry-go-round

I feel very dizzy

We have two days

We have only two days

Time to trust in Jah and

let him handle the rest

Trust in Jah and he'll handle the rest

I feel like I'm letting them down

I can't let the people down

I have to accomplish ten things at once

Can't stop to examine my thoughts

Woke up and caught a jitter

The feeling crawls up and down my skin

Like a critter

Tapping my thumbs

Scrolling through Twitter

My coffee is black

It tastes bitter

Sparkling & shining

I'm glitter

Leaving this broken building

I'm a quitter

Electrical current running through me

I'm a transmitter

Stomach Knots

Prince Harrison, Jr.

As I'm writing this

My stomach is in knots

Twisting & turning like a Twizzler

Sold my soul for something fleeting

Broke down in my bed

Chaos in my head

Can't forget what she said

Déjà Vu

Prince Harrison, Jr.

This has happened before

This exact situation has happened before

It happened last year

It happened this year

Oh, if only I could return to the past & fix my mistakes!

If only I could focus on my spirituality

If only I could focus on something else

If only I didn't care about people

I wish empathy didn't exist

Can't Breathe

Prince Harrison, Jr.

My mind is dizzy

Left side of my body hurts

Got yelled at today

Lost myself

They gossiped about me

Made a group chat and all

Dragging my name through

the mud like a frog

I'm sick

Tried to hold on, instead of letting go

Don't know how to talk to them

Don't know how to talk to them

Falling in love

      Falling in love

           Falling in

                  Fear

I apologized

Another relationship ruined

Another child without a mother

Another empty trash can

Another liar

Another fire

Another broken heart

Another tragic experience

Another toxic wasteland

Another reputation ruined

Another reason to never love again

The Feels

Prince Harrison, Jr.

Hurting someone can be as easy as throwing a stone in the sea. But do you have any idea how deep that stone can go?

— Unknown

I have no idea why I feel these emotions so strongly

Someone hurts a person, and they forget

Someone hurt me, and I can't forget

Anxiety tells me to write it down

I'm slowly falling down,

        down,

        down

Can't pay attention

Can't focus

Can't breathe

Had a few panic attacks

Cried a river of tears

Got depressed

Felt like someone ripped my heart outta my chest

Felt betrayed

It hurts

Felt bitter

It hurts

Felt crazy

It hurts

Felt desperate

It hurts

I don't think I'll ever be the same

Anxious Soul

Prince Harrison, Jr.

Everyone is out to getcha', getcha'

Intrusive thoughts squeeze the life out of you like an anaconda

Nightmares become dreams

Dreams become nightmares

You wake up with ominous music playing

Nothing is there, but the music is playing

Nothing is happening and you shake like a blender

Can't turn it off

With each day that passes, it gets more severe

Can't focus on yourself

Gotta help the others

The others leave

The anxiety doesn't

It's still there

It's a ghost that won't disappear

A phantom that laughs in the background

Feelings broken

A golden token

My soul is lost

in Hoboken

Take It Away

Prince Harrison, Jr.

Jah,

Please take it away

Take away my ability to feel other people's pain

It's too much

Take away my ability to write poetry,

I'd rather sit on the sidelines in peace than continue writing in agony

Take away my ability to think

I'd rather have blank thoughts than chaotic ones

Take away my empathy,

Because it'll never be reciprocated

Take away my caring spirit,

Because the world doesn't care if you want to help

Take away my focus,

Let me use it on something else

Take away my panic attacks,

I can't control my emotions, so I need closure

Take it all away,

Send me to Mars or Pluto if you have to

I feel cursed with talent

I'd rather have none and just exist

Let me finally be able to live a normal life

It's all I've ever wanted

What Won't Break II

CC Miller

Click and lock

Lock, stock, and barrel

The narrow escape from the pain

Convincing in its anxious desperation

That breaking

will

be

BAD

Too bad to bear thinking about

The thoughts too loud

Cloud judgment

Pushing options off the table

Breaking will hurt beyond survival

It's a lie

We recuperate

My Darling, we weren't born to die

Regenerate

Procreate

Populate an earth that heals

What

Won't

Break

Built to Break

CC Miller

You might call it a calling

The bereaved won't grieve for me

Too tired to count the tries

I count a collection of reasons for my being,

Many a time, the sole survivor of something

my soul should not have survived or

something perilous disproportionate evil exaggerated the score for

My hero needs no hyperbole in mentions

I accept my saving-grace on faith that I'll make it

Because he always makes it up to me or

He makes me up to it

Being afraid is a decision I'm afraid to make

The density of the faith in what many see as fantasy,

Opaque to me

Too fantastic to skeptics and dreamers alike

My mind walks over matter

Like my Messiah walked over water

You don't know the lengths I'd go to see the light

I wasn't created for this but for His sake He makes me

Built to break

Instincts extinct for self-deprecating traits

Playing small less I fall and see humiliation

Camouflage can't conceal threats from his vision

Even the ones I present to myself are exposed to him

I can take a break

He builds me up from it

Like a conjugate verb

Doing what's possible in his might

Because he is predicate of my predilections

I fail into flight so when I'm falling

You might say I'm soaring

You might even call it a calling

Fatigue

CC Miller

Laundry to be washed, to be hemmed, mended, or scrapped

Comes out of my ears and overflows

Filling my lap

Onto the floor

Up against the door

A great pile of washing, hemming, mending

Washing against the walls

breaking in waves

An overwhelming, tiresome, incessant

Not sure when I wore that

Where I wore it to

I don't want to offend if I should mistake

so, I wash it, too

Wash the regret with apologies

The stain of it relentless

Wash the odor of old habits

Soaking in new patterns as needed

Hemming for my height

Not too much

Not too little

Take out an inch off my pride

Let out an inch for my esteem

Dieting and exercising means

Constantly adjusting me

Mending never ending

Not sure if it tore from snagging on something sharp

Or if I just outgrew it, pulling it apart

I can't have things spilling out indiscreet in places

Meant to be personal

It's a tedious, tiresome, laborious routine

With a reward immeasurable

Fresh with a sunshine scent, a conscience clean

Polish and Shelve

CC Miller

Prettily you sit for eyes to ponder,

and woes forget

Prettily you take the elements, the dust,

the light, the polluted noise of critics

Readily accessible to be touched

To be held

To be withheld

To be taken down, polished, and shelved

The Boring
CC Miller

Your eyes are boring through me today

Only in my head can you torture my breaths

The seriousness of you shades me

A blushing shade that warms my insides

with a mix of something nameless plus shame

No profitability to missing your boring eyes

The hopes you scorned linger on

Haunting visions

I'd wish me embittered

Rather than trailing thoughts of your eyes

boring into me

Looking into my recesses like that

Merely scoring my impenetrable

Where others left scar tissue

In irritating tickling

It isn't necessarily you I'm missing

But the boring

The boring of your eyes

We

CC Miller

We have dreams that don't act their age

Smiles that don't cave

When we're together

it's atomic

When we're apart we're together in thoughts

That match like outfits we wear on our inside voices

So loud I hear your lol in my inner ear

Even though you text it

And I knew you meant it

Not unlike when you text that weird grimacing grin face

I know it means you forcing it

Whatever I'm trying to get you to go along with

You really ain't feeling it so I acquiesce

And we do something different

And it's cool

Cause I pro'ly ain't want to do it anyway

I mean, it's best we do that another day

Our textures fabricate tactile

Playin' with the fringes of our comfort zone

Because we both about that spiritual expansion

Exponential growth

We tag team and push the envelope

Our favorite game

In the name of all things good and happily ever after like

Natural sympathies

a symphony made for infamy or eulogies

Whichever comes first

But we flirt with forever

Foregoing all kinds of things that matter but don't matter

A pattern of lost winks

Cause there's too much to lose if we lose the fight with sleep

When we say things we really don't mean

Like good night

When we say it for the 17th time

Goodbye

Cause the minute we're out of one another's sight

We make excuses to question one another's minds

Like, *I was just wondering*

Really absolutely useless nothings that mean

I treasure you and you cherish me

Did you eat

As if I ever miss a meal

It feels good to miss you, though

even as I kiss the neck of a nickname between us

Knowing spoiled but not rotten is a delicate balance

A top spinning nonstop onward

You feel loyal to my dreams

Till you've got my nightmares scared of your cross hairs

It seems I'm in the kind of trouble I like

Again, for the first time

Cause my heart acts brand new 'round you

Like it ain't ever let the silver light of the moon see through

Slivers I couldn't fill with anything less eclipsing than you

Anyway, you know what it is you do

That's why you haven't asked me to fill the quiet in the 2.5 minutes maybe three

That I've stared at you in the talkative silence

Coy

Bashfully

We

Small, Low

CC Miller

Eyes out the car window

Voice small, low

He said, *"I'm bred to be head*

I've bled for those I've led

My mistakes carry a heavier weight

There are no ears for my complaints

I know they're waiting with bated breath on me to do something,

say something

great

But

What if I cry

When I try to deny myself

I should say provide myself an escape of the energy crisis pent within me

If there's an intensity, I may not have the strength to contain

Rain might ask my pain to waltz

A masquerade bawl of grace

Small

low

A wall of gritted teeth brick layer a crescent on its back

Fulfilling generational contracts that demands be met

to hang the moon with duct tape, a hair pin, and a tack

Attacked and bashed by voices that vet black boy joy

A declaration that the other noises need silencing

Or risk emasculating

So be a eunuch by force or be a eunuch by choice

I'm told inspired expressions of demons that this is all at the hands of Jezebel type women

Out of my control

Feeling small, low

Knowing when to hold 'em, fold 'em or walk away supposed to come naturally

When no one before me collected that history in libraries of my community

What if I die at the hand of a clumsy tongue, venomous

Rage misplaced

Impetuous tempest

Youthful ignorance matured into willful petulance

A vehement viper with vicious malice in mind

Dismantle the masculine in heat of adrenaline

Small parts present a choking hazard

Low expectations do the same"

Saying this in a saltwater language

One that I happen to know

Staring through water and window

Small, low

When They Go/Rubber Boots
CC Miller

Soggy astonishment doesn't light fireworks

But you ran into the rain of bitter disappointment

with only your admiration of things that fall down

and a pair of leopard print rubber boots

Without let up

It poured sour over your sweet

It sloshed about your feet

Pruning the skin raw 'round toes that just love wiggling in those rubber boots

And you keep staring up through raindrops for stars

Things that stay fixed in the wonderment of hope

Things that always stay

Even when they go

Confidence

CC Miller

Adopting the floods

Relatable deluges

In my confidence

Peace

CC Miller

It's that powdery blue that isn't quite
Leaning but not committed violet
Sedating manic drumlines of deadlines
Marching dandelion thistles on wind
Winding gently on a summery flight

It's that powdery blue that isn't quite
Playfully pursuing the dancing fawn
Beaches not peopled except by the dawn
Bathing in every sensibility
Gratefully rinsing away hard feelings

In that powdery blue that isn't quite
Seductive quiet that begs more silence
Coaxes intimacy out of hiding
Swallowing whole a rich, decadent peace

In Dreaming Color...a Compilation

Ashley Wooten

WAKE

I dreamed of you last night and didn't even realize it...I just thought you should know; you are already my normalcy.

Schizophrenic symptoms seduce my sanity because of your wonder. I wish I had multiple personalities so we could meet again and again. The time you spend with me in my dreams confuses my reality. The only reason they call my mind a thing of beauty...is because of you! 😉

N1

I don't believe in magic, but you are a true MAGICIAN.

You've made dust from nothing

Defined a dust-nothing as a dust-something

Inclined the dust-something by blowing your holiness into its nothing nostrils

And as that holy breeze entered into this dust-being,

I'm sure Adam sneezed

N2

Please. Have no pity for poor lil me. Pouring constantly into a special teacup. Custom porcelain, handmade...only one per earthly being... We just so happen to be unlike anything ever seen by humans. This special teacup transforms me into a specialty...a mixed drink of sorts. I am no longer what I was before. No longer afraid to over pour. Because I'm mixed up with you.

You are the finest port wine ever created. The content within reveals a past and healing; it's all in the base. You pour so beautifully and not a drop of you will go to waste. Even when the puddles become emotional ravines, your…our drink offering will remain in the holiest place.

N3

How come the clouds mimic the mountains' unlimited-ness?

I had a dream we built sandcastles in the middle of rushing waters

We decided to define them as a ravine of feelings.

We are an island in the sense that I land perfectly where your treasure chest rests.

In the heart of our beach.

Breaching love whales wail and preach sonnets especially for you and me.

Before I forget, I adore you too! I'm not sure if you actually said the phrase but your actions prove how you feel. You're unreal in even your own dimension. So just think of the havoc you're causing in mine. There's no such thing as time when it comes to you and I. That's why for us twilight is the best time. Know why? Because the black backdrop gives us the night sky to shine. In our own little play. I love that my night, loves to visit your day. 😊

REM

Imagine

A world with no borders

The four walls of forethought formerly fortified under Fort Knox

Now forced to box with forgotten corners of my mind

In my world, there lies

Cordless camcorders pre ordered since the beginning of time

Which means...my eyes

Re-corded re-porters who reorder and re-mortar memories solidly re-sorted in the slumber phase.

This place

Keeps me blinded by the light of day

And still

My eyes have faith

And so, they say

If seeing is believing

Then believe me...

I'd seen you way before your eyes ever knew

Who knew?

That you would be.

The dream that Jehovah allowed to come true!

Reality won't break my dreams

One for the Team

Ashley Wooten

I don't want to **_break_** your heart

by

allowing you to break mine

when

I know you're not ready for me…

I won't allow us to break

Sweet Life (Time's Past Pictured)

Ashley Wooten

I have these photographs,

 the memories...

These Polaroids preserve our

pretty cool

Pretty full

Pretty life's

Pretty petty

Sometimes

How a pretty penny only pays for

candied dreams now

Oh man

Remember those penny candies!?

1 cent sent me all the way to the sky

and back.

Bliss prayed and paid for

I've got plenty of proof to prove it

A cavity space filled with a paper trail of pictures in it.

The white borders shelter our white smiles

undenied true happiness at its best

I love that album

I'd pay with all the candies and all my teeth

To document that sweet life again.

Time won't break memories

You're the "-EST"

Ashley Wooten

The way you listen...

Let's me know your heart

The way it beats confuses the highest human beings and their colleagues

You're so cool

Your magic is everlasting even when you go away

I hate when you go away.

But if you stayed, I know I'd take for granted this most missing-est piece of my heart's beat,

my heart skips beats better than Dre's for

Beating the oddly satisfying pacification phase.

The absence of your absence is the only true thing to pacify me.

I can never get the right words

To write the right words feels wrong-est

When the strongest of my feels be

The longest story I ever loved

To live

I live for your beats

The heart of it responds the most-est

You're the dopest

And I just realized I said that line wrong.

I love for your heart

I mean I live for its beats

I mean I live for your heartbeat

And I know you don't live for me

And we both live for the highest being

But I love to live in a world where the simplest breeze reminds me of your

Rhythm and Blues

Or the Jazz.

We bleed the same in the middle

Our middle names tell it the best-est.

You're the freshest

Have I told you that before?

I probably have

I try not to think about it too much

You tell me when it's

"Too much, too much, too much, too much"

Too much too smitten with you

So, I'm the smitten-est

Test me out please

Like my God requests of me

And I'll prove

Not to be a goddess

Or the god-est

But I'm definitely a modest reflection of his Godly recollection

If ever you question

My love for you

My friend

Always remember

The effort it takes to just chill

Remember how natural it is to fill one another's space…

Lol respectfully

And then you'll see how unnatural

It feels to only have the trees rustle

And a breeze

Without your actual

Heartbeat

Because of your heart, I won't break

Encounter

Ashley Wooten

Were you waiting for me?

For how long?

But like, when did you find the time?

You trade a smile for a reply

Eternity lingers in your eyes

And at the top of your brow

An eternity, it seems to be

It is that you waited for me

But you tell me not to worry

That time is too infinite

And infinity is too long to

assume a pit stop to my moon

Illuminates your stars any less

And inspire them to extend into forevermore

Our galaxies will always combine

Just in time for you to wait for me…

yet again

Our bond will never break

At All Costs

Ashley Wooten

Porcelain dolls don't have eyes that shine like yours. Their transparency clarifies the mystery of eternity. Turns "misunderstand" into "understood". Still here I stand. While my self-centered wishes strike your iris. They take in my shadow's space and embrace my face. In an instant they shrink back and make the blacks on the whitened background look like dollops of the purest love glue, the perfect cure for shards of shattered heart glass

Congratulations! Your porcelain eyes have crashed into my unspoken broken heart. They are guardians of my mental milky way galaxy. Amazing how much I worry about vehicular accidents now. Must consider the statistics on car crashes and keep control of my megabyte count; because your eyes create traffic, fill up photo inboxes and remind me of what we truly live for. To be thankful.

Porcelain dolls invite and deny their ability to be touched, like you do. Confuse onlookers who are memorized by your smile, those cheeks...those teeth. How dare you! Be so cute, so sweet. I hate that I wish at times I could be blind so I wouldn't be able to see you blink. Because it terrifies me to think that when you sleep those porcelain things have moments to dream. Makes me rather jealous. I hate I can't see the sky in your eyes or that something other than my fingers protects you when you cry. I can't say I've ever been here. I can't say I've ever cared so much. Never worried about the pollution people must breathe, concerned about solving crimes of why people sneeze, I even look at trees differently. Simply because of your stare.

Unaware of a bond that never leaves. We are bound and bonded, I am in bondage when you look at me. Locked in love without a fitting key. All I mean by this is...I am a boat that sails only on dreamer's seas. Those salt waters happen to be your tears. I promise to protect these waters at all costs.

No

Hurricanes,

Earthquakes,

Zealous cyclones, not even

Your own mistakes

No:

Lightning storms

Opposing rains

Gigantic tornadoes

Avalanches

Not a thing, will keep your protective buoy away.

You and your porcelain eyes will last the test of time.

Auntie's got you.

I won't break your hopes and dreams.

Creation Space

Ashley Wooten

They don't know that we already know

what they'll never really know…

that it usually takes a lifetime to recognize how the little things hold the beauty.

But not for us.

God is in the details, baby.

The architect of the greatest pick-up lines.

The way a wink is formed because of the sunshine.

The natural smile of a crescent moon…no wonder we swoon for creation.

I already know that you know this, but I'll say it anyway…I love you baby, and nothing will take me away.

<u>Love don't break</u>

MEND

Breakfast

Prince Harrison, Jr.

Eggs & grits

Bacon & fried fish

Pancakes buttered with biscuits

Onions minced

Hush puppies silence hunger like a librarian

Fresh Floridian orange juice

Straight off the trees

Strawberry smoothies with toast

Yum, yum, yum!

These words fill my heart with glee

A perfect way to start the day

Breakfast for me

Break Away

Prince Harrison, Jr.

I need to run far away
I need to run far away
To my safe haven

Where I can break down in peace
Where I can break ice like a shovel
Where I can break hearts in my head
Where I can destroy neighborhoods
with my hand

Where I can inspire people to love
Where I can break society's norm
Where I can break the status quo
Where I can go against the grain
Where I can break roots of a tree
Where I can turn cement into concrete
Where I can play with your emotions
like a guitar

Where I can use my words to change your brain

Where I can write poetry like Shakespeare

Where I can break clouds like an airplane

Give me a chance

Just one more time

Let me sing the praises of Jah

And break away from the sins of mankind

Duplex III: Bleed in Emotion

Prince Harrison, Jr.

I was born to bleed in Emotion

The neurons in my brain cause chaos & commotion

My brain is scrambled like a broken puzzle

I can't seem to find my calling

I can't seem to find my pen

Her ink is beautiful, it reminds me of calligraphy

Bleeding in ink, my emotions are calligraphy

I can't seem to control them like most of you do

I feel things the strongest, I'm not like most of you

You will read this poem and shed a tear

I will re-read this poem and shed a tear

I wish I could stop caring about people

I wish people would start caring about me

It's time to re-wire my brain

It's time to put out the flames

I was born to bleed ink in Emotion

Yesterday Night

Prince Harrison, Jr.

I got on my knees & begged her to stay

My lungs are colder than an ice tray

My lungs are full of cold water

I sent her a message last night

She ignored my message last night

Called me strange for going back to her

Called me strange for missing her

My heart is treacherous & desperate

My body drowns in treachery & desperation

Told me she was sorry I felt that way

Told me she was sorry I'm a failure

She took a sword & stabbed my heart

I pleaded with her not to damage my heart

She laughed and cut it with scissors

My paper-thin heart gets cut by scissors

A broken boy that calls himself a poet

I'm a broken boy; but they call me a poet

I knew it wasn't going to work, but I tried anyway

Knew it wasn't going anywhere, she departed anyway

I'm on my way to the doctor

Crying & bleeding, I call my doctor

She tells me it's all in my head

They always tell me it's all in my head

I often wonder why I let her in from the start

Memories choke my windpipe, my car won't start

All we need is time to heal this emotion

Wasted my time & I can't heal my emotion

I got on my knees & begged her to stay

Some People

Prince Harrison, Jr.

SOME PEOPLE COME IN YOUR LIFE AS BLESSINGS, OTHERS COME IN YOUR LIFE AS LESSONS

— UNKNOWN

Some people

Come into your life

To break you

And

Some people

Come into your life

To build you

Never Forget

Prince Harrison, Jr.

PEOPLE WILL FORGET WHAT YOU SAID, PEOPLE WILL FORGET WHAT YOU DID, BUT PEOPLE WILL NEVER FORGET HOW YOU MADE THEM FEEL.

— MAYA ANGELOU

I'll never forget

How you made me feel

I forgive you

But you made me feel useless

I won't say you're evil

We're all imperfect, so I can't blame you

Some of us are selfish, I can't blame you

I'll never forget

How sick I was

I'll never forget

The tremendous amount of pain

I'll never forget

The emotional trauma

I'll never forget

Feeling empty

I'll never forget

How can I forget?

Some people are so mean

I stay quiet and observe the world around me

Life goes on

Time heals all wounds

Mankind's sins will one day be forgotten

Princykins

Prince Harrison, Jr.

I take all the negative energy around me

And absorb it like a sponge

I transmute it into poetry

I can read people's emotions like a book

I try to make them feel better

Because I know how it feels

I know how it feels to be alone

I know how it feels to be broke

I know how it feels to be lifeless

I know how it feels to be heartbroken

I know how it feels to be deceived

I know how it feels to be worthless

I know how it feels to be misunderstood

I know how it feels to be sick

I know how it feels to be hopeless

I know how it feels for life's anxieties to kill you slowly from the inside

I know how it feels,

Yes, I know how it feels,

Let me help you through my words

Let them be of comfort to you

Let Me Heal

Prince Harrison, Jr.

Jehovah,

Give me the strength to heal

Give me the strength to push past this traumatic experience

Give me the strength to keep moving forward

Give me the strength to serve you in more ways than one

Give me the strength to fight for my blessing

Give me the strength to make it to the Paradise

Give me the strength to control myself

Give me the strength to run the race to the finish

Give me the strength to do better in your service

Give me the strength to become a good example in the congregation

Give me the strength to keep being myself

Give me the strength to risk trusting people again

Not everyone is out to get me

Not everyone is out to hurt me

There are people out there that actually care about my feelings

Please find them for me

Give me the strength to look past it

Give me the strength to pursue spiritual endeavors

Give me the strength to heal

Please, let me heal

Amen

Forget-Me-Nots
CC Miller

It might be considered a small favor
Mine were the kind of wounds that didn't break the skin

The wounds within
Mine to mend

Inhaling colors of sun, rain, and wind
Tattooed beautiful blue forget-me-nots
Camouflaging spots
purple from the disregard for my soft

A perennial blooming spread
 promising to remember and respect
How tender I am
And how tough I am

For mine were the kind of wounds that didn't break the skin

A spoken burn deprived satisfaction the oxygen of reply

A lie contrived

 lit like it was a kind of kindness

A favor bestowed upon the mindless

My wounds know no worse fate than festering untruths

Half-truths spread ugliness

Ignorance, an abuse of bliss

A disrespect to the conscious

The sulfur scent of the unspoken verbs

more unpalatable than the acidic words

I tattoo new beautiful blue forget-me-nots

A mural memorial to all that I will be and begin

It might be considered a small favor

Mine were the kind of wounds that didn't break the skin

Loud and Clear
CC Miller

I hear you loud and clear

You want me to get over it

I'm grateful that it means you're tired of me hurting

I love you for that

Imagine that I love me, too

Imagine that I want me to stop hurting more than you do

Imagine that I can't imagine how to

Without giving up the love that opened the wound

Imagine that I never want to give up that respect and love and joy

Now imagine you asking me to

Some things hurt because they've no choice but to

We've been tasked to endure

What we were never meant to

Some get by by closing doors and locking up rooms

I prefer to visit all the memorials

Touching all the tender places

Remembering why I miss the impression of expressions in empty spaces

Thinking of them warmly

Letting them wash over me in watercolor

Wall papering them fresh so they never fade to sepia

Kodak to Polaroid to Nikon crisp

So yes, the pain is sharp, but the love is rich

And nuances of me clutching the thing that's cutting me

 is a small price for something priceless

Imagine that I'm reckless because I cannot imagine being careless with them

Because even if I am not the one they want to,

they will always have someone who treasures them

Imagine having no one or so few to treasure you because it cost them a tear or two

Imagine that I never want to give up the admiration, the laughter, the meaningful nothings of love

Now imagine you asking me to

It Fell

CC Miller

My recollection leaves out the part that starts with
what I was doing

It must have been thoroughly engrossing, but
The heart stopping moment when
                        it
                          fell

Like watching the early days of cinematography
starring myself
in 3rd person

And the precious miniature figurine that I knew not to touch
An amateur stop motion film
Tumbling to the floor
Eerie little frozen smile stuck

Mocking the fear icing my veins

Unbothered by its fate

as it couldn't know where it was headed

Taking so long to tumble

as if it could slow down the minutes

So many heartbeats till impact

The sickening clinking sound of ceramic snapped in two

The little bits too fine to mend like new with glue

An unutterable gasp escaping by a chain link of tears

The heavy kind, that drag

As if I, myself, had cracked

"It fell," I said, through the thickest tears

Because of the shock of it

That is all that I recall

None of the prelude to the fall

So, with a painful familiarity

You have always shared with me

I understood

When you could not put into words

What you should

How we arrived here

Snapped in two in a sickening clink

On the floor of the end of what seemed

Like an interminable fall that was truly over in a blink

An irrevocable break

"It fell"

Patting my person down to be sure I was all there

That pieces of me didn't need salvaging

 from the wreckage

Vowing to God not to ever again be so careless

With his precious things

Spirited

CC Miller

Resilient, indomitable, persistent

Intangible properties of the human spirit

Things only proven in defiance of diminishing them

Defiance, rebellious, radical

Spirited

Fruitage

CC Miller

I took my Love for a walk

Faith dawned on my skin

Highlighted my best features

A glow of Kindness

A youthful Goodness

A dewy Joy

So mesmerized with the shine

I lost Self-control and tripped over discouragement

A distraction meant to cripple Mildness

Patience called for Peace and got me back up on my feet

Divinely Architectural

Ashley Wooten

Words of wisdom are the best.

Gives the gift of reminiscing about unforgettable looks with smiles in them.

Hastens kindness and makes anger slave to my satisfaction.

Makes the sky blue with a hint of pearl.

Makes the soil look like chapter books with once told tales

About how my mother,

 laid under blades of grass, gracing the ground with black silk from her head accompanying her.

Ageless feet propped up by the wind.

Gratitude humming through each toe and the breeze identifies them for their own personality.

It makes time seem to tick in reverse,

 backtracking to places with abandoned memories waiting for a spectator.

To look, to see, to learn.

Is to leave no fleeting detail untouched.

To earn the right to be wise,

Is to touch the fringes of the highest power's garden,

Edenic creatures meeting you there,

And your access be granted...

for eternity.

Heaven on earth, actually.

Godly wisdom...unbreakable faith.

In the Days That Follow

Ashley Wooten

He sighed a little too loud that time.

A sign of knowledge.

That he broke my heart.

He undermines my disguise of resilience

As if a mannequin could mime me more brilliant

I'm not broke

I'm just broken

In the most put together way.

This golden heart of mine,

A retriever of

rich wishes witnessed in past tense; withered,

waving within a winter's blizzard of tears.

Stormy weather is natural

just nature's way to cry.

I dry them up…

Fear's tear-flakes…

The future's forecast,

An exit stage left of us acting as our own cast

Because of him,

I don't cry no more.

My heart froze

Anger don't try no more

To hide

No more

Mind games

No more

"I've changed"

No more believing

Because trying to see the best in you

Means deceiving myself.

The best of you is the best,

And the worst part is that the rest of you is fleeting…

Like scattered leaves retreating from an autumn breeze,

Fearful that they'll catch cold from the cold.

Your hold on me, like those leaves have died off.

And now,

Resting peacefully is the cold, cold truth.

The truth that I'm fine without you.

I am fine.

It's just that my face doesn't know it.

Okay, so

I'm not fine...

I'm a bit broken.

No more leaves to create a shade's cover

But other than not being fine,

I'm great!

Just a little bit damaged.

Days will pass and bare trees will sprout their truths concealed

The breath of life will take over and a tree of healing will be revealed

In the days that follow

Even broken hearts keep beating

Wish You...Well,

Ashley Wooten

Broken wishing wells only seem broken when your wish doesn't come true. Lovers throw currency into brick and mortar, black abyss with hope and pleas that this token makes dreams, even the uncanny ones a possibility. It's my bad for wishing for you.

Broken wishing wells only break when your faith in them dissipates. Therefore, the callousness of hurt burns my heart every minute and every second of the day to admit I never relinquished the hour in which my wish came true. I would plead for my heart's frequency to strip, rewire, complete the missing circuit evidently evading your eyes. Look at me. If only in your dreams. From the part where you said you loved me more than the two sugars in your black coffee to the secrets you thought only to yourself. The ones only meant for hearing in twilight, during your extra 10 minutes of sleep.

And I must apologize in advance for the potential nightmares you may have of me. Compassion is something rather blinding so I make sure I can always see what I'm getting myself into. I'm so sorry I'm not able to yet hold you.

Wishes won't break you unless you let them...still, I'm sorry

OMW (On My Way)
Ashley Wooten

Good morning

Good afternoon

Good evening

And goodnight

1,440 fresh minutes trapped inside this hourglass of imperfection

Correction

86,400 seconds destined to deaden me in a quick 70 or 80

Cheers!

years to

Dropping my body in the sands of time

Buried deeper than fossils and geodes alike.

So far away from the light of the sky

But to answer your question

I'm doing fine

I happen to be great

I am an earthen vessel that has settled to the bottom of an ocean of the world's tears

And even down here

In the evening part of this sea

I see

the right hand of something beyond this world

Something holy

Something heavenly

Something

Somebody

Whose hands only eyes of faith can see

Racing to scoop me up and sift out all of my impurities

And there

is a black diamond

Roughed up by the fruitless pebbles that surrounded she for so many

hour's

broken glass shards don't

Make his hands bleed

Don't need it

The blood

His son dived for the whole team

So, these hands

digging deep

Call me a treasure

Says my value is worth dying for

Ever, next stop

X marks the spot

On the top, bottom, and middle notch

Beating these imperfect odds

So here I am

On another day

Of

Good mornings

Good afternoons

Good evenings

And goodnights

On my way to

Forever

…My God's grip won't break

The School of Scarred Hearts

Ashley Wooten

To whom it may concern,

I take it back. Everything I said. I'm sorry. I must've misread my heart once again. My heart. She's led me to make the same mistake. The one of telling myself that a heartbreak is enough to make me a better mate. Telling me a heartbreak can show you how to maintain self-love. It can re-create and reincarnate a feeling of self-worth.

See a heartbreak will decide for you; happens in order to liberate you. Unequivocally erasing the sheltered, unidentified, unadulterated and underestimated hole where his place used to be.

This black space sucked me dry. Drains the colors defined only in the darkness of my mind. Makes it truly dark there. Decreases the mention of my broken eyes, my pretty teeth, I forget me…In a heartbeat… Of a heartbreak.

A scarred heart won't break…me forever

Meek Matter

Ashley Wooten

I wish freckles speckled your face. So, I could count the constellations that shape a handmade creation of my God's grace. My God. How beautiful your traits would be placed upon his nose, on both cheeks, and for me, my God how much of a blessing that would be. Maybe connecting those facial plains could keep my attention on something other than my imperfections. Connecting the dots could map a path to his heart and just maybe I could understand how just one ventricle could love me.

Passing thoughts won't break the truth

Thumbs Up

Ashley Wooten

I'll admit that I cried myself to sleep last night. A Heart shaped stain was all I left as a river of endless ache trickled down the tip of my nose to precipitate finally off the front of my face. Supplication gets me every time. Because the want and need to be okay only reveals itself succeeding the acceptance of things not being that way. So swollen shut are my eyes. My ability to breathe inhibited by self-commiseration. Silenced by the hiccups lodged in my throat. The kind that are so embarrassed of my gift of emoting.

I admit I cried myself to sleep. Last night. I cried for what seemed like the first time. A liberation of feelings exceeded the point of no return. Soothing the dark copper that is my skin after it had been burned raw. An inner bomb ticked until an explosion arrived, making a guest appearance for my familiar guests to guess what I had fallen from. To hurt like this, I must've fallen. How could I have missed that!? Falling. Forgetting. Amnesia doesn't dismiss the fact that something is missing. But I did. I missed it. Missed every comment I ever made. Missed the pretty portrait in words that I gave to almost everyone who deserved a bit of color in their gray. I missed a step up on the way to an insane sanity. I have tripped, stumbled, fallen and was stricken with the fact that.... that I am just right. Just enough, and not too much. I am a present and someone's future. I am the gift that keeps on giving. I make you better. I make things worse. I am worth the fight and priceless all at the same time. Mind body and soul, I'm a wholesome girl...and that's okay!

I've done so much coloring in other worlds that I missed the haze that fills mine. But yesterday, well last night, I finally cried for what seemed like the first time. And for the first time...in the heart shaped stain I saw the colors that make up...my make-up no more makeup to hide that some days are not okay and that's okay. I'm okay. Just enough and not too much and that supplication along with those tears of thanksgiving enabled the forgetting and the forgiving that I needed to realize, to really see that I have the only true God, beside me. So, I'm okay.

Let's break the misconception that "not okay" isn't okay

Untouchables

Ashley Wooten

There is a guild built on a foundation of dreams

At the top,

live specimens whose occupation

 is to weaken, tease and buckle limbs too shaky to stand still

Heart be still

Knees be still!

Please, for goodness' sake

For dignity's sake…be still, stay shut and be quiet.

These beings belong to a penthouse devoid of dividends, no requirements of monetary value needed here.

You must employ though, what I say,

What we say, what they say is a type of commodity.

To clarify one must be eyes embracing sunshine, illuminate body, rays pinpoint,

anoint and target my center, their center, our epicenters of sentiment.

Your audience must approve of the message you send.

You must be…

Untouchable to me.

That's what they're called,

In our minds,

Not out loud, we'd never say,

Out loud the things we pray for in our apartments, underneath a compartmentalized barrier, in a department of unrequited panhandling, seeing only the *couldn't-possiblys*, the *shouldn't-thinks*, the *never bes* see we've established a society too.

We be bespoken, belonging to them, secretly.

Just as untouchable as those who rule our very moods.

As distant as our future with those beings in their penthouse. So close to God.

So able to choose whoever they want to.

I heard a poem the other day, it was so sad, and so true.

This charming midwestern swoon whose name would make you think she had spurs on her shoes, she said something about striking a match in the void where a spark of light should be.

She tried to force a dream to be a reality

I.e. you

An untouchable

You know who you are

And it's okay

We've already bespoke our pride to you.

There is a guild whose purpose isn't on purpose.

A Divine accident of sorts

They've been built on dreams,

They're meant to be real,

Only here,

Before we sleep, in the darkness of an empty crowded room.

Wide eyes closed shut

Tears overflowing into pools

onto pillows too full to comfort

Us,

awestruck, lovesick, forlorn fools.

Us!

We're fools

because we forgot…

While attempting to fabricate a place in the hearts of an impossible race of beings we forgot to gaze upon a beautiful physical estate.

Our own!

We extend our limbs out for a mortal vision's embrace and still haven't respected a reflection for brilliantly repudiating self-hate.

So how about we flip the script and redefine some things.

If we only reasoned appropriately, we'd see

We be bespoken already

Closer to God than any penthouse can achieve

Worth more than all the dividends, expenditures, our bodies out body paragraphs etched with pencil paper and pen.

We can choose exactly who we want and then choose again.

We be beautiful, we be brilliant, we be bound only to the love we give we

And so that means we be untouchables now!

And anyone attempting to touch me,

Must first reach in grab both shoulders and accept the person that they embody.

Receive the love you need from you boo.

Bask in rays made to illuminate; strong body, kind eyes, reasonable mind, accept Holy Spirit.

Jehovah God made it for you!

Only then, can your untouchable dreams really, fully come true.

Since you're untouchable, you won't break

What You Need (Short and Sweet)

Ashley Wooten

I don't wanna be

different,

I wanna be better

Be better at being better, not being the same by trying to be different…don't break your personal growth.

CLOSURE

Breaking News

Prince Harrison, Jr.

CNN, BBC, MSN

More terror for me

More sadness, violence & pain each and every day

I'm tired of watching fellow man

kill fellow man for money

I'm tired of watching children get kidnapped

I'm tired of schools being shot up

Malls being shot up

Blood spilling on the floor like milk

I'm tired of this corrupt government

I'm tired of the UN

I'm tired of imperfection

I'm tired of depression

I'm tired of action faking

I'm tired of the hating

I'm tired of two-faced people

I'm tired of the loquacious ones

I'm tired of fake peace

I'm tired of singing the same

sad tunes over & over again

I'm tired of the anger

I'm tired of the deceit

I'm tired of watching people get beat

I'm tired of the sorrow

I'm so tired of the lies

Jehovah, please rescue this world soon

And bring about the Paradise

Brake

Prince Harrison, Jr.

Let's slow down

We're driving way too fast

Maybe it's the gravel

These roads remind me of the past

We were going 100 mph

Straight across the Brooklyn Bridge

Ignoring the traffic

My soul went cold like a fridge

I took the wheel

And slammed my foot on the brake

Breathing a sigh of relief

We nearly made a mistake

What Won't Break I

Prince Harrison, Jr.

What won't break

Me

What won't break

Us

What won't break

Brothers

What won't break

Sisters

What won't break

My spiritual family

Despite threats

Despite trials

Despite tribulations

Despite attacks from the nations

We will remain steadfast

Immovable

We won't break

Duplex IV: Fill That Void

Prince Harrison, Jr.

I was in love with her instead of with myself

I stack the memories like books on a shelf

I throw the lost memories in the trash

She forgot about me and moved on

I forgot about me and moved on

I dreamed of her in a black dress on the beach

She wore a ripped black dress & I woke up

I'm drowning in an ocean of loneliness

I'm drowning in an ocean of infatuation

She's not real & I can't stop thinking about her

I'm trapped in the Matrix, and I can't stop thinking about her

How do I solve her problems?

Why can't I first solve my own problems?

I need to focus and limit these distractions

She was my main focus & she's a distraction

I was in love with her instead of myself

Duplex V: Break Me

Prince Harrison, Jr.

The last thing I needed was motivation

It's time to express my vexation

Vexation fills my arteries like blood

You tried to break me & didn't succeed

I'll take the success and break free

Smooth seas can't make skilled sailors

I'm a sailor in the middle of a hurricane

Good things take time to develop

This is my time to develop

Painful suffering always makes me stronger

What doesn't break me will always make me stronger

I'm a sky full of dreams & some are far away

I reach for my dreams because they're far away

Great things come to those who wait

Great things are coming, my blessings await

The last thing I needed was motivation

Duplex VI: Building

Prince Harrison, Jr.

I look at the pretty duplex house

I aspire to take it all in, and espouse

I aspire to build a duplex that strong

Brick & stone grow on one another

The duplex poetry form builds on itself

How did they construct such a beauty?

How do I construct a beauty?

I practice the words and they build on themselves

Sentence fragments & similes build on themselves

They're built the exact same way

I start with stone & they go their own way

The grass is green & the lawn is mowed

The grass stays green because it's a "Rent-To-Own"

A foundation so strong, it can't break

My foundation is strong, I won't break

I look at the pretty duplex house

Loss & Leaving

Prince Harrison, Jr.

I never handle loss very well

I remember when a baby died

I remember when an elderly sister died

I remember when a basketball star died

I remember when a musical genius died

I remember when I almost died

I remember when she left

She's not coming back, Prince

She's not coming back, Prince

She's not coming back, Prince

She's not coming back, Prince

She's not coming back, Prince

She's not coming back, Prince

She's not coming back, Prince

She's not coming back, Prince

She's not coming back, Prince

She's not coming back, Prince

No matter what you do

Your Bubsy is never coming back, Prince

Apologies

Prince Harrison, Jr.

BAND-AIDS WON'T FIX BULLET HOLES

— TAYLOR SWIFT

Sorry won't fix her

Sorry won't fix me

Sorry won't fix the pain caused

Sorry won't fix the house caving in

Sorry won't fix the debacle

Sorry won't fix the memories

Sorry won't fix the current situation

Sorry won't fix her true intentions

Sorry won't fix my true intentions

If Sorry won't fix it, what will?

Jehovah.

Caring Too Much

Prince Harrison, Jr.

Anxiety-driven

Caring too much

Trying to detach

Can't detach

Give people my heart

And they stomp on it

Pull the rug from under me

Beat me up

After they're done

They move on with their lives

Scars On My Aorta II

Prince Harrison, Jr.

She broke my heart and I found me in the process

I gave her my all, and she was thankless

Gave her more and she thought of me as less

These tears I cry are inevitably in vain

These tears I cry are birthed from pain

She told me she'd never hurt me

She hurt me & lied that she cared

I was the only one that put forth effort

My efforts were for nothing, she left

Gave this pain to me as a gift

This pain is truly a gift

For I will use it to write like never before

Heartbreak isn't forever, I was weaker before

This experience made me stronger

This experience made me more mature

She drained the blood from my aorta

My aorta still works, it found hemoglobin

My heart still works

to paradise I'm going

After all these years I finally found me

She broke my heart and I found me in the process

Artist

Prince Harrison, Jr.

We only ever care about the art

and never the artist

I write most of these words

When I'm suffering

And turn them into something you can enjoy

Something that you can relate to

Something that can make you stronger

I realize not everyone has the courage to do this

But if this life taught me one thing, it would be that you should help as many people as possible

Build a legacy

Make an impact

Create something that will live on

Go

Prince Harrison, Jr.

Let it go

Gotta move on

Gotta keep pushing

Gotta keep on and carry on

The camel's back is broken

A new dynasty is in place

Let it start a new destiny

How far will I go?

Far in life

To places that people have never been

I'll help the people in need

I'll care for how people feel

I'll mend the broken hearts

Jah will forgive me for my sins

He'll fix my mistakes and make me strong

I have to keep going

The show must go on

Can't Break Me

Prince Harrison, Jr.

> WRITE YOUR HURTS IN THE SAND. CARVE YOUR BLESSINGS IN STONE. —UNKNOWN

In this life, people will hurt you

You'll be kind to them

And they'll repay you with evil

You'll give them a place to stay

And they'll stab you in the back

You'll protect their feelings like a jewel

And they'll crush yours like a soda can

You'll let them into your life

And watch them rob you blind

Despite the disgrace,

Despite the shame,

Despite the pain,

Despite the hurt,

You can't break me.

Despite the thievery,

Despite the emptiness,

Despite the tears,

You can't break me.

Despite using me,

Despite losing me,

Despite playing me like a fool,

Despite pulling the rug from under me,

You can't break me.

Despite throwing a Round Rock,

Despite pink crocs,

Despite shiny silver spoons,

Despite books,

Despite Austin,

You can't break me.

Despite tricking me,

Despite sour candy,

Despite seafood,

Despite ladybugs,

Despite the similarities,

You can't break me.

Despite the FaceTimes,

Despite your wicked lies,

Despite spilling my secrets,

Despite Togo,

Despite Passion Twists,

You can't break me.

Despite Strawberry Ice Cream,

Despite the moments we shared,

Despite the memories lost,

Despite the potential I saw in you

Bubsy,

You will never

Ever

Break me.

Forward

CC Miller

BeLoved, forward is the way home

Forward is where you belong

The person you were when you were last there

doesn't exist anymore

You couldn't go back even if you dared

Go forth, BeLoved

Dismiss the doubt

Deconstruct the myths

Know with every bead of sweat

You've got this

Yours, Wholly
CC Miller

        I wasn't ready for you not to want me whole

         It was a thing I couldn't have prepared for

                         me

                   for

             up

For you to see me stand

        Knowing the fight behind me

And feel compelled to sit

              me

                  down

Well,

       If having me at eye-level is uncomfortable

        I sincerely hope there is a pill for that

            For I intend to rise

          Whole and uncompromised

Absence

CC Miller

I processed your abrupt absence
 like I would a book or movie ending
It happens

People's absence
I would've liked for you to be a force
A presence

A cadence to depend on
A friend on into millennia to come
There are no sequels for us

Our characters parted ways like death does
so, I mourn you

(Take that with salt
I mourn the ending of a plate of food
If it was good

I mourn summer even though it'll be back again

It makes sense that grief would leave
a calling card where you had been)

Your absence stacks on racks of remnants
All of you are Absent Man

I can no longer distinguish you from the others

sometimes I retreat to dreams where you appear
Stitched from his arms
His shoulders
His eyes
Your ears

Only the parts of you that were mine
So very Frankenstein
I'm not sure it isn't a nightmare
But you're there

A moving picture

Awake, your absentia reduces you to apparition

The plan was always to love you
In some construct
But even though it doesn't need it
Love likes to have permission

Recognition that without permit
It must stay outside production

Counterproductive to proceed where it cannot succeed

It recedes to reels of footage that picture nothing kept
Just film flapping against spool absent of images to project

The Best Thing About a Breakup
CC Miller

The best and worst thing about a breakup

is that everything won't break up

You can't break ties with the time spent

The nagging wonders

where it could've gone and

knowing where it went

Since time is a house we never sell,

We rearrange its furniture

and introduce new smells

We hang new drapes and wallpaper

Fill it with sounds of new stories we tell

But when all is said and done

We don't go back to being our pre-union selves

There's no way to unlearn your SO

He will always know

that she puts the sun in time out

between 10 and three in the summer

But behind open blinds

Carefully observes the year-round rain

and keeps a watchful eye on winter

a sharp ear for thunder

Not so much a weather voyeur

Just that she always expects the worst

and prefers to look it in the eye,

so, it won't sneak up on her

He'll never forget she hates surprises

And

She will always know how he does

or doesn't hold his liquor

The interpretation of the shadow of his brow

when he doesn't speak up

Not so much a desire to be a mystery

as a self-imposed prisoner of his history

These are things that might alter but never change fully

A can of legumes can dredge her gut

And dreadful distrust lurks behind every flirt

But washing behind her ears can expose all her teeth

And while the thought makes her cringe

He doesn't shop for honey anymore

because he can never look at it the same way again

And she knows this

And he knows why he gets annoyed when he can't find the red tie

even though he can't remember out loud why

And he hates this

And he married quicker than he wanted to

because of that thing she said one time

The thing about a breakup

And she married later than she wanted to

Because of that thing she learned from the last time

The thing about a breakup

That everything won't break up

No matter how hard you wish it would

in a way we are a fraction

a duplex formed from picket fence dreams

Moving around artefacts of the past

Like someone rearranges furniture, it seems

Because the new tenant of her heart won't know why

her nostrils flare at his red tie

Like they're in a bull fight and he is a new hire matador

And she a bovine

And his new lady roomie won't understand why, when it rains,

 he stands in the open door

With that stupid grin on his face

That's only stupid because he won't tell her what it means

And her new him won't get the aversion

to him being in the kitchen

When she prepares a meal

He'll write it off as a women's control issues or,

if he's smart, her prerogative

But he won't know that in either truth he's only partially correct

Because both of them are just renovating a house

That's built out of what's left

Because the thing about a breakup

Is that everything won't break up

Including her small voice when negativity is loud talking her worth

And her self-respect

Now, that stays intact

Unless God himself is pulling on it

And he will never lose another good thing again

Because he now holds a whole comprehensive education

on the economy of demands on a good woman

His conviction complete that he will forever man up to the challenge

Of falling perpetually in love

Because the thing about a breakup

Is everything won't break up

I Would Like to Love

CC Miller

I would like to love my way

Open as each new day

Welcomed like morning sun

Warm, giving, generous

I would like to love in spades

Plentiful as flowers in May

Bubbles, iridescent

A patient refreshment

I would like to love a fiery blaze

A passionate rain

Gusts of butterfly guts

Every shape and form love comes

I would like to love like me

And so,

I do

We Were Pretending

CC Miller

We were pretending to be finished

Graduates of kid-dom

Masters of our futures

We were pretending to have figured out fears we never saw coming

We broke rules in the pretense that grown-ups don't use them

We made mud pies of friendships

Set them on asphalt to bake but never ate

Because ew

We treasured our imaginary friends long after we told people that imaginary friends were stupid

Yet we were wired to them

Willing to live and die for them

We blew the breath of life into them if ever a glitch should keep us apart

We played god

We fantasized adulthood to be some kingdom we would all reign in

When it rained inside, our castles were all built of and on sand

But we rebuilt them in short stories

"When I grow up", we said

Insert lack of introspection

Irrespective of the narrative we spent all that time perpetrating on ourselves

Because we pretended to be grown

To make ourselves whole from broken homes

That were everyone's norm

And no one's throne was ever good enough to remain sat upon

But we would not be deposed

We moved on from places we never left

Most of us became what we dreaded

Some of us learned the trick to sandcastles is

a little more distance from the ocean

And a little more patience

And some of us still have imaginary friends

Even some that don't come wired to obey our commands

But they do what we say anyway

Because in our make-believe world,

fake is perceived to be anyone who won't

and still walks around okay

Anyone who knows that being grown means the rules were the only way

to get there safe

Not that we aren't pretending, too

We just know that's what's happening when we do

Like, how in this minute

I am writing myself to okay but I'm afraid

My mom will see it in my face

She'll know that I'm not there yet

That I'm not grown and I

Am just pretending

What Mattered
CC Miller

What mattered was what I thought we meant

The time we spent on the investment of us

It mattered that we stockpiled trust

That the currency of glances and the language of wicked smiles was always good between us

What mattered was that I always fit like your favorite pair of jeans

that you never wanted to lose, give, or throw away

No matter how distressed they became

That I always knew how to read the skies of your irises and tell the season

What mattered was that our life lessons put us in a class all our own

It mattered that I always saw the hourglass horizontal

when I heard your laugh

That hoarding a warm honesty would always be our habit

That we would make a hobby of collecting reasons to stay

It mattered that we would bend together or apart

But never break

That we would only take what we were eager to give

It mattered that we would live

It mattered more that we would have a life than that I or you had a life

It mattered that we would live

What mattered was that we knew one another well enough to preclude what we didn't know as a transitory adventure

Like restaurant hopping on weekends

What mattered is that every flavor of us was our delightful favorite

That fragrances of our touch would mean total recall of a time

And place that belong to our little community

That we would be family

What mattered was that that could be the only thing we knew was certain

And we would be satisfied in its abundance

The relevance of everything pivoted on what mattered

And matters still

Railroaded

CC Miller

My veins transport transcontinental tribes and clans

like train tracks tote other man-made constructs of the same transient nature

I conduct myself in a state of wonder at which direction my freight of fright and fight truly hail from

Am I to hate some part of me as if I am to have my own blood asked back from me

As our Lord and King equates hate and murder as the same thing

I'm not suicidal lately

once upon a time, I stood up from graveling at the mercy of oncoming locomotive lights and

dusted my backside of the gravel

Addressed the court with the only gavel that matters and pleaded for freedom from being railroaded for misdemeanors

Those I had and had not committed yet

As I have only ever spent time in the caboose of time

my intentions are to outlive its usefulness

Insurrection won't resurrect a bloom from the seed it died from any more than a bullet can retrace its origin

Whereas I vowed to a bond with my redeemer

where release on my own recognizance was simply not possible

I abandoned the nomadic life of a hobo for a forever home

where all of me is welcome to freely go

No more about to let what's in my veins determine how I train

than I am about to let this metaphor runaway with me

Not taking for granted that there are those who have managed to let the sound of the men working on this train derail a brilliant and vibrant fleet of people who look like me

I simply don't concede defeat to centuries of attempts at upsetting peace

I worry less about what is commuting in my veins and more about the train leaving my brain

For out of the heart the mouth speaks

A universal language of love

A global track that runs forward and back

Like infinity

Where my veins are full spectrum network of forever and family

Of Willows, Reeds, and Dandelions

CC Miller

The willow heard from the reeds
 the dandelion was an invasive weed
The low country song from a percussive beat sounded true
for it was sweet

The reeds knocked against one another
Bowing low and bounding tall
The dandelion, so very small,
Sang no song
None at all

As her petals began to fall
The willow felt strong in her resolve
To believe the rightness of reeds repetitive song
A head of delicate, white
in place of its yellow crown

And willow wailed ever louder,

"See what reed warned and heed,

The dandelion be a useless weed"

One by one, as wind would blow

Thistles from dandelion's head let go

Dancing on a high wind's heels

Lying to rest in distant fields

Where reeds song might not reach them

New dandelions would there grow

Blanketing the fields

in the brightest yellow

Yellow for teas, for salves,

for syrups and things

For the jewelry of cherry-cheeked princesses

the headdresses of ladies

All so helpful for easing pain inflamed

For bringing easy delight to a dreary day

Over time, in generations of windy days

Destiny would fade away

The song reeds played, that willow sang

But Dandelion would find, forever, her place

See You (Meditation on Job 14:14,15 and John 5:28,29)
CC Miller

It's not that I don't remember you now

I just remember you to the God of the living

That means the days gone are a moment paused and not stopped at all

I will see you again

When the death certificate was signed

I resigned that my only power lied in detached doing

Moving through motions methodic, morose

Moreover, misanthropic mechanics meant my suffering made a home in service

where I was safest

distant

Not too far for you to love or leave me

Bitterness bought time from better habits for years after to make up for this

I was so used to being stolen from myself that I joined what I couldn't beat and became my own thief

Till belief claimed my name and released me

I'll meet you on the other side of sleep

Where rivers of peace will greet us

Where we will be ruled by the open hand of love

And justice like we've only dreamed of

Our joy will be complete

On the other side of sleep

I hear your laugh and see your smile

And I ache for it to come from you

Knowing it'll be just a little while

Till that prophecy comes true

When you awake from the deepest sleep

Refreshed, young, and new

Responding to Christ Jesus' voice

There I'll be to meet you

It's not that I don't remember you now

I just remember you to the God of the living

That means the days gone are a moment paused and not stopped at all

I will see you again

When you fled home

A refugee from protection

I heard your absence echoing the eviction

Your haven unsafe

quaked for days

A cognitive dissonance not strictly of the brain

gave me a stern reminder that emptiness aches

like nothing else

As you were exiled, I opted for asylum

None can extradite the prisoner of a war within

Anointed womb a disappointed tomb

Wept blood while denying the welts

Whatever that took away from reality was worth the price or so said my mind

Being on house arrest to one's body can incline one to serious misgivings about what's real

I asked to be released on my own recognizance as much as I knew reality would never again be a friend

You precious martyr

You don't sleep in vain

My reason to reach for the ransom

which I up till then rejected as too rich for my taste

I placed my hope in rehab and you in God's hands

It's not that I don't remember you all now

I just remember you to the God of the living

That means the days gone are a moment paused and not stopped at all

I will see you again

2015

Ashley Wooten

The hardest thing I think I've ever had to do,

is keep my hands to myself.

 Because the next breath in your chest

 I want, I rather, need to catch it.

 I can't understand how someone's breath can mess up the me inside myself.

Be the death of my best but the life to my desperate health.

 If only for the defined disease that needs to please and test the faith I have.

Choking my integrity.

Like how can your mere presence attack one's entire playing field?

Like corrupt the true purity that stains my brain

like bleaching and dying my thoughts to think another way.

You're winning a game I was never taught to play.

Train me, please?

Excuse my lack of shame

and excuse me for not wanting to explain,

and me trying to explain,

and me over-explaining

and me still not attaining the punctuation at the end of this supposed sentence.

This **broken** sentence

This unending, barless sentence.

See you've murdered my common sense.

The punctuality of your arrival has slain and maimed my body to move in a way that would be diagnosed as "clinically insane".

In a proposed sentence,

if my body were the words and your voice was the pen

I, then, grammatically, would be completely incorrect.

But,

you expected that didn't you?

Knew exactly what to do when you saw this college shoe-in.

Knew my purpose when I picked up a pen. Thought to yourself

"She pro'ly has a journal,

bet my name resides the most within.

if it isn't, it will be"

I can almost guarantee you planned to make an already written book empty again.

Attempting to transcend an unintentionally extended and already ended event…

you know make it begin again.

Like this poem.

See, I lied.

I can control my hands.

Denying oneself is how I revive my integrity.

Pounding the chest cavity until its rendition of the song it seeks lulls you into the melody u spin.

Your turn tables unable to turn the tables of sin.

And since you play a game you can no longer win,

the poison from within now unleashes its tormented grace,

my resentment now etched in your face, and as you wipe it

you're beginning to fade.

My journal no longer has a home for you, she said you can't stay.

It may be time for you to close my written pages and create a better actor for your play.

So next time,

you may actually win at your own game.

My integrity won't break

Life lesson #6

Ashley Wooten

Entry #6:

Never expect more of someone than they expect of themselves.

Their actions will always show what they feel they're worth.

But your value is not measured by their decisions.

Time will tell the truth for them.

We won't let your worth break

AOA (Alive on Arrival)

Ashley Wooten

I caught a body 👀

Did you hear me?

I said I caught a body...

I said I caught a body in a bottle on the waterfront today

I mean I got a bottle's body as I fished it out of the San Francisco Bay

With a message that I wrote to you.

The clouded glass matched my composure as I pried open the top

Unsure of the condition of this lost past that came back to me

You came back to me

Coupled with waves rushing as

 fast as my memories did

As soothing as the waters end and the sand's Genesis

Exiting inhaler patterns

Patterned to fit my lungs

I think it's time to inhale her again

Rather me

She

Her/me/she

You get it

Gen Z got us speaking more specifically nowadays… 😂

And it's not even their fault

But anyways

I digress

Gently pressed and preserved in this glass un-shattered reserve

Was and addressed letter, only afforded to be whispered in the sender's breaths

She told herself

Remember you're a human being and imperfect

And that your feelings don't need to be bottled

Set off your emotional throttle

Let the layers of your prayers explode from the belly of your chest

Better yet

Do the opposite

PUT those emotions in a bottle and send them away.

Ashley, when you've grown and truly know yourself,

And are for sure you're okay

Go back to the Francisco Bay

Catch your body

In your bottle

And let the seaside

Wash those tears away.

Breathe her in again.

My body won't break

Quiet Storm

Ashley Wooten

Shhh...

Mic drops

I stop

Eyes lock

Dear God

Prayer off

10 knocks

My thoughts

Run hot

You need

time off.

I opt to

 just not with you today.

The audacity you've birthed!

To think that your inconsideration deserves an open place in my heart's open space.

I think

you've got

it wrong

No song

Can make up for this quiet violence.

I shall let you hear yourself in my silence

I can't believe it!

You take my kindness for weakness

And my silence for agreement.

Don't mistake

Yourself

My worth wealth

Be bequeathed

To a Queen

Best believe I'm not a peasant heiress

In a white dress

We made so many memories before this.

And that kiss we had the day I do

released family tree names

To create one anew?

This branch barely balances you

and me

today.

Okay.

I just grew

up

Different.

But instead of letting this bough break...

Ain't nobody fallin'

But that couch can cradle that head

And all of your yawnin'

Lol good night

Those thoughtless words won't break me

RIP-Psalms 4

Ashley Wooten

I've got loyalties in a special way. (V3)

Thankful that I am loved and heard.

Especially on the days when the wickeds' absurd words become too much,

And they hover like vulture birds, clouding my sunny day.

Sometimes the righteous say them too…

…our friends say them too…

But I buckle down and do what I'm supposed to.

Although I'm agitated, I promise I won't sin. (v4)

I tell myself this over and over again…

Because my loyalties need to stay loyal in a special way.

I can have my say,

 in my heart,

I'll go to bed, and

Rest In Peace.

A cool breeze hastens to wake me up.

And although the foolish will still be

clinging on to a worthless ruse,

They call it life,

peaceful and secure.

I'll be good, and secure too.

Basking in the Sunshine that is your beautiful face,

O Jehovah.

No father is loyal to me like mine.

You fill my heart to the brim with joy.

That's why it doesn't bother me that the wicked, the bad boys, toy with my emotions.

Because,

because of you,

All I need to do is,

Get in bed,

Bow my head,

And loyally list out these things,

And R.I.P.

What hates me won't break me

'A Note on Love.' Inspired by the Homie of all Homies

Ashley Wooten

10:22am: Text message from a good friend. "A note on love: 'If it's your first real love it never really dies. What actually happens is that either your hurt or pride grows bigger than that love. @vidatherapy'". "Oh dang, lol" she says. I ask if she agrees. She says, "I was trying to let that marinate and I guess so! Or I wonder if it can get replaced with a different kind of love? I don't know, haha!"

 A side note, I hate conversations with this friend. I have to pretend like I'm not amazed at her timing. Try not to feel obligated to say the most inspiring things that come to mind; she makes me think. So, I make the best rebuttal I have: "I think it's both. Or maybe a progression. U love. U leave or get left. So, u hurt. Ur heart and pride are hurting. So, u let ur pride heal ur heart. In the process of that, ur pride tries to override ur heart's pain so u act like u hate. U grow. Chapter gets closed and u realize u never stopped loving. And although u don't love the same, the having love part never changes. First loves will always be loved."

Love can be a sign of completion. But also show a distinction between a lover and her feelings. It can provide electricity of the purest kind. Be a hand to hold when the electricity dies, the end of the mental stimulation. It can re-current a warrantless circuit known only to be infatuation.

Apologies, there's been a misdiagnosis. These are just true feelings in simulation. A placebo of emotion. Real life bleeding doesn't even hurt this bad. Doesn't sting as much as when that hand she held for the span of their eternity lets go without a choice in the matter. Heartbeats scatter in her ears. Over and over again all she can hear is the sensation's surround sound replacing her thoughts, the reasonable ones anyway. Overthinking leading to what if's? Why nots? Why hers. It hurts for sure. True love though, never fails, right? Right.

Our fears won't make us break

UNBOUND

Unbreakable

Prince Harrison, Jr.

Every story has

its hero & its villain

It depends on your perspective

Real life doesn't fit into

little boxes drawn for it

Sometimes these events occur for the

sake of justice

Sometimes we get hurt for the

sake of justice

Sometimes people die for the

sake of justice

Sometimes people live for the

sake of justice

Sometimes people rise to power

for the sake of justice

Sometimes people disappear into hiding

for the sake of justice

Sometimes people sacrifice everything

Their bones

Their limbs

Their sanity

For the sake of justice

Daybreak

Prince Harrison, Jr.

Day breaks & Night falls

The Sun rises but it also sets

Dusk becomes one with Dawn

And Moon & Sun agree to be one

Stars unite with Fluffy Clouds

And Fireflies & Mosquitoes dance like ballerinas

Morning takes the place of High Noon

Duplex VII: Breaking Windows

Prince Harrison, Jr.

We break the windows of their duplex

We take stones and throw them at the river

We take stones and shatter glass

Shards sprinkled on the ground

The ground swallows the sprinkler

They said there was nobody inside

There was a baby inside

She had beautiful brown eyes like my mother

My mother told me to capture beauty

She told me to look for the helpers

I am one of the helpers

I busted the windows and saved the human

I break down windows in order to save humans

Some of the trauma still lives on their tongues

The pain resides on the tip of their tongues

We break the windows of their duplex

Duplex VIII: Breakthrough

Prince Harrison, Jr.

We break through the walls of gold
We spare the children and the old

We take the children to the old playground
A wide-open field, grassy and divine

Divine and grassy, it reminds me of Savannah
A juicy Georgia peach rolls under the table

Rolling hills fall under the black table
A story swathed in vines from the forest

Red wine we steal from the golden forest
A tribe calls for the bodies of men

A prostitute calls for the bodies of men
She is met with disgust, and runs away

Our hearts cry in disgust, we're runaways

We declare war on the inferior people

Our blood sheds tears with the native people

We break through the walls of gold

Duplex VIIII: Wildfire

Prince Harrison, Jr.

You lit a flame and started a fire
The families are full of rage and ire

A container full of rage and ire
Smooth words spread fast like butter

Lies spread fast like a disease
Gossip is only so innocent

Gossip is ever so guilty
A pretty girl with nasty behaviors

A pretty girl with evil intentions
Her pearly white teeth trick the people

Her teeth are swords that cut deep
A house engulfed in flames

A reputation destroyed by flames

She adds fuel to the blaze

The trees add fuel to the blaze

You lit a flame and started a fire

Duplex X: September 2027

Prince Harrison, Jr.

I'm at the altar but I'm all alone

My bride won't even pick up the phone

My bride was supposed to be here today

I don't know where she is

I don't know where the love is

The time we took to have our future planned out

Our future plans are up in the air, time is running out

What was I even thinking?

What was she even thinking?

Two crazy kids that magically fell in love

One crazy kid falling in fear

She finally shows up, but she's not in white

She finally showed up, but she's not my wife

No need for the ring, cause she's with another

No need for tears, I comfort my mother

I'm at the altar but I'm all alone

Her Perspective

Prince Harrison, Jr.

He tried to turn me against my friend

That was the day where he met his end

That was the day where I ended things

I was sick & tired of him bothering me

I was sick & tired, he still tried to reach me

Claimed that he was just checking in

He was not just trying to check in

He tried to manipulate me & my bestie

He tried to turn us against each other

I blocked him on everything & moved on

I blocked him; gotta focus on school & spirituality,

Wish I didn't lie to him

Wish I didn't meet him

I made all these promises that I couldn't keep

He made all these promises, that he planned to keep

I told the other girl about his intentions

The other girl knew about him

Thought he was a player

He's a manipulative psychopath that's a player

He's lost his mind and I don't want him in my life

He lost his marbles, called me his future wife

He tried to turn me against my friend

His Perspective

Prince Harrison, Jr.

I wish I could tell her I'm sorry

She ran faster than a Ferrari

She ran faster than the speed of light

Wish I could explain this misunderstanding

All of this is a gigantic misunderstanding

I truly care about her feelings

I asked if she was okay; 'cause I still care about her feelings

I made the mistake of telling her

I wasn't aware of the mistake I made

I'm sorry for messing up badly

I'm sorry for messing up this badly

You told me to "leave you alone," and I will

You told me "Have a good life," and I will

I hope we can smooth things over one day

I hope we can hug it out someday

I'm just thinking of what I could've done different

I could've done anything else, you would've been indifferent

I tried to diffuse the situation

I always try to diffuse hostile situations

What I did was dumb, and I now realize

I was young and dumb, now I can look at you with real eyes

Father, Father, forgive me for my sins

She's gone & now I'm grieving

Protagonists always grieve the most

I wish I could tell her I'm sorry

Like I Used to Before

Prince Harrison, Jr.

I don't like you like I used to before
I planned a future for us, it was fake
Gave my love away like a toy
I need to prioritize myself this time
I'm always chasing after the wind

I don't like you like I used to before
I'm sick & tired of feeling this way
The truth is the hardest pill to swallow
Silly me for biting off more than I can chew
When will I learn to stop caring?

I don't like you like I used to before
I'm sorry, writing it down is the only way I can process the pain
This sentence is stuck in my brain
I've been cursed with anxious energy
Was it even real in the first place?

I don't like you like I used to before

The trauma makes me codependent

What will it take to fully love myself?

At least she was honest this time

I don't like you like I used to before

My heart is extremely naive

Did I ever even like me?

Pain is the only way to grow

Don't cry for me, I froze my heart and threw it in the snow

I don't like you like I used to before

I put her on a pedestal and I'm paying the price

I can't even taste my favorite Jollof Rice

I always go the extra mile to make others happy

I blame it all on me

I don't like you like I used to before

I daydream about things that will never happen

I don't want to be liked again

Don't even want to look at her, don't want to be her friend

I don't like you like I used to before

This is the final time as I've come to learn

I won't ever be loved if I can't love me first

I'll take these words and bury them in my heart

My self-love journey I'll joyfully impart

How many more will tear my world apart?

I must leave this tragic state, I must depart

Liar

Prince Harrison, Jr.

I ACCEPT ALL PARTS OF YOU, THE GOOD AND THE BAD. I'LL ALWAYS CARE FOR YOU.

– BUBSY

Oh, who would have predicted this outcome?

She said she'd always care

She's a liar

This one hurt more than all the other ones combined

Gave her my all & she stabbed me in the back

Twisted the story & turned it on me

I feel numb

I feel used

I feel embarrassed

Why can't we humans be honest with each other?

My emotional intelligence trumps common human nature once again

She pretended to care about me

Like a lion pretends to nurse an injured deer

Haven't felt this low since my attempts

Haven't felt this low in years

I feel my stomach in my lungs

I can't move them

I feel paralyzed with fear

Who's truly at fault here?

Her or Me?

Me or Her?

Maybe I should take some of it for believing in people

She told me not to break her heart

And I didn't

I told her to not break my heart

And she did

Ironic

Gave me the whole "it's not you, it's me" speech

Dropped a bomb and left me stranded

Lifeless on an island

Swimming in an ocean with infinite waves

Father, Father, I pray that she matures

Her lies made my soul insecure

Jawbreaker

Prince Harrison, Jr.

IT'S NOT LOOKING TOO GOOD FOR YOU, PRINCE

— HER FRIEND

My mind plays these evil tricks on me

It tries to fix these problems, even though they don't need fixing

Can't leave a situation alone

Feels like I need to help

To make things right

To try & salvage something that's irreparable

Shrapnel hurts me

Arguments upset me

Girls won't break me

Broken Bubsy

Prince Harrison, Jr.

I'm sorry

I wish I could send this to you

but we no longer talk anymore

And that breaks my heart

To feel this sadness so strongly

Makes me feel weak

Wish it didn't have to end this way

Wish it didn't have to end this way

Wish I could've made you smile

Wish you could've made me smile

Wish we didn't hurt each other

Wish we didn't yell at each other

Wish I could've given you more

Wish I could stop thinking about you

Why can't I stop thinking about you?

I know that you hate me now

I know that things will never be the same

I realize that things are over

But my mind can't move on

The pain sits on these words I write

Wish in our last moment; I could've said goodbye

Wish I could control my emotions

Wish I didn't have to cry every time

I think about you

Wish I didn't have to grieve

Wish I didn't know how to write

Wish I could switch brains with someone

Wish I didn't have to be anxious in this life

Wish we didn't meet but

We did

Wish we didn't like each other but

We did

Wish we didn't have heated exchanges but

We did

Wish I would've cut it off in the first place

I tried to salvage something unsalvageable

I tried to save something that is dead

I tried to excavate an empty casket

Wish we weren't so young and dumb

Wish we weren't inexperienced

Wish I could stop thinking about

that day in June

The day I met you

I remember when you graduated

How happy you were

How happy I was

And I sent you a gift

Actually, made it two

You couldn't decide which one you liked better

I think it was the Duplex I wrote

I remember

When we shared stories till the late AM

I remember

When we shared pictures

The highlights of our lives

I remember

The FaceTimes

I remember

the goodbyes

I remember

The check-ups

I remember

You waking up early

I remember

Me staying up late at night

I remember

Us quizzing each other on Bible stories

I remember your laugh

I remember your gorgeous smile

I remember the passion twists

I remember the beautiful ocean pics

I remember me being out of pocket

I remember

the day you went tubing

How happy you were

I remember the pink dress

I remember the Austin picture

I remember the pink crocs

I remember planning to visit Texas

I remember trying to sneak to Omaha

I remember the aspirations

I remember picturing you as my future wife

I remember saying I was going to marry you

I remember you calling me crazy

I remember you calling me crazy

I sound crazy for writing this down

I remember the dancing videos

I remember the Truth or Dares

I remember you crying

Because I went to sleep early

I remember waking up early to comfort you

I remember you dreaming of me

I remember the TikToks

The Togolese, Ewe, French,

Poetic connection

I remember your love for poetry

It was potent just like mine

Your work was as beautiful as a rose

I remember your cute little southern accent

I remember you giving your return visit

in a black & white dress

You called it a "side profile"

I remember when you attended my Bible reading

I remember when you said we were a good match

And I believed you

I remember when you said you'd never hurt me

And I believed you

I remember when you said that

you'd care for me forever

And I believed you

I remember when you said that

I checked all your boxes

And I believed you

I remember when you went to Galveston

I remember when you invited me in service

I remember when you told me how much you cared

I remember when you said that you didn't care

I remember when you said you

gotta focus on other things

I remember when y'all started talking about me

I remember when your friend attacked me

I remember me apologizing for me being hurt

I remember trying to make things right

I remember everything going wrong

I remember you calling me a creep

I remember you being selfish

I remember being lied to

I remember being deceived

I remember leaving you alone

And you thanking me for doing so

I remember the day we first met

You had meeting that day

I had meeting that day

It rained

I took a picture of the scene

You asked if I wanted a PFP

I said, "yeah"

We played iMessage games all night long

It was so much fun

We had so much fun

Saying goodbye is always hard for me

Because I simply never stop caring about people

Even when they hurt me

Even when I get attacked

I just have a big heart

My anxiety calls me a **Brainiac**

I remember when I told you my secrets

How Depression X Anxiety haunt me

Daily like a ghost

How you said you'd check on me

I called it infatuation

You called it a lie

I called you self-absorbed

I still don't know how to say Bye

I've gone through denial

I've swam past the anger

I've ran past bargaining

I'm stuck at depression

I'm stuck at depression

I can't move to a place of acceptance

I'm sick because of Mooshu

Woke up and caught the flu

She's stuck on my mind like glue

Wanted to take her on a baecation

in Peru

Met her in June

Her eyes were pretty like the Moon

Lost her in the desert dunes

My one true love gone too soon

What about this poem?

I guess it has to end

I can't cope with the pain

And I can't pretend

I'll remember how I cried today

And how I turned my misery into art

The chest pain still persists

Because Bubsy broke my heart

Storyteller

Prince Harrison, Jr.

Let's end things on a happy note
Let's end things on a happy note

I tell stories to touch your heart
I tell stories to touch your heart

These words I write find their way to your heart
In deep oceans of Azure, I find me

Deep oceans don't scare me; I finally found me
What if I told you that I'm happy now?

What if I told you that you can be happy now?
Hold onto Jah & he'll make you strong

I hold onto Jah, and with him I'm strong
I pray that I can be in the paradise

I pray that we can be in the paradise

We'll tell stories & cry tears of joy

We'll finally be able to cry tears of joy

I hope to see you there

You will definitely be there

Don't ever, ever, ever let this world break your spirit

Don't let it break you

In Flight

CC Miller

Pray I fly on humble wings
Truth be my thrust and lift
A gentle trust to harshest wind
Feathers preened by goodness

Pray the sun grant my flight
That an exchange of light permit
That clarity pierce darkest night
And patience be my plumage

Pray I break into song
The sky duets my solo
As I fly on bowed wings
Ever so very humbled

Amalgamated
CC Miller

shadows of ampersands tug

Anchoring my heart

so that I can't surface

my oily wings tread in watery wishes

Repelled by my nature

it's alright

I'm creative

And learn how to physic

A light to scatter shadow

A binding agent to bring water to the sun

Determined to amalgamate

Dreams and reality into one

Sound Barrier

CC Miller

Sounded perfectly thrilling

Approaching the speed of sound

Hope echoes resound

Acoustic acapella

36,000 feet up

Compressed or concussed

It could only be wondrous

Magnificent just

My depths to be heard by you

Not only the heights pursued

To have you present

as I express this

An exhalation

Caught by your inhalation

Hopeful, ignorant

We reached the sound barrier

Flying faster than safety

I Wasn't
CC Miller

Memories filling my head with the details you're privileged to forget

Sharp, vivid

A drowning in my own fluid

Re-feeling the language lingering

Longing for lopped off air

Your laugh lapping against my lungs

There

Where you were remembered and

I wasn't

Cutting Remarks

CC Miller

Serrated knives fascinate

Pretty scallops and points intrigue

But what they do to the meat

What they do to the cheese

Loving the sharp edge doesn't polish it round

It shreds the spirit beneath the flesh

It can't right what's left

In the time it takes to see it begin to make headway

It makes grotesque the beautiful thing

Misery of majesty

A gift used for bloodguilt

Gilded lily dripping red

Millimeters by milliseconds

Bled by the thinnest laceration

From the body's smallest blade

Abrasion

Heady in its pursuit of harm

The vile and small

Cutting remarks

Cracks in the Sidewalk

CC Miller

Compacted, pounded

Truth raining soaks, transcending

Cracks in the sidewalk

Gravel and Glass

CC Miller

His voice dragged open

Wounded wishes well-deep

Chords of gravel and glass shards

Tore through scar tissue

Rubble and debris

Articulation ties hurt

and slurs staccato pain

How can it be so

Gravel and glass dragged slowly

Leave cuts unseen

Bleeding meaning

Gaslight
CC Miller

Other than the faint hiss of friction

There's only one sound

Ignition

A spark converts butane into open flame

And it all goes up

Every recorded date, transaction, meaning

Every understanding

All that made a name

Angles, lighting, shadows shifting

Twisting truth into twilight zone screenplay

Dreamscapes glitch

An awareness that the matrix is collapsing

On itself

Confused whether this is red or blue

Wires cross and boom

An explosion rewinds you back to you

Reminds you of the you you knew

You

Demand that they acknowledge there is no spoon

Hiss

The sound of a fingerprint across the ridges of the wheel

Shake your head at the glitch

A squeaky hamster wheel comes into focus

You notice you know this should be a wheel

But what and why a hamster?

You inhale deep to center

Hiss

A Ferris wheel?

The deception gets so comforting

You just might be confirmed

Who would be hurt by lying down with this lie

Who would be victimized

if you let a deception bless someone's recollection

Carve creditors from debtors and

Enslave a free man

Hiss

Gaslit

Breaking point
CC Miller

Hello

And welcome

To your breaking point

An exclusive Last Days property

Here you will find your vestigial last nerve

It may be difficult to identify so, for your convenience, we've marked it with acute pain

Beneath your triggers,

The delta of your paycheck and bills,

Your employers' cognitive dissonance when it comes to work life balance

And your bodies allergies to aging

There it lies inflamed to high heaven

To make it easy to find

Your family, at your breaking point, either believe you super or subhuman and persist in testing both theories relentlessly

For a limited time, you qualify for a buy-one-get-charged-three upgrade to basic necessities of life

If you act now, we will throw in priceless luxury lifesaving prescriptions to keep you here at your breaking point for as long as possible

Except they will, of course, be priced

Exorbitantly

These can be financed at 100% interest on the Kuwaiti dinar (not the US dollar dear)

We are an isolated and secluded property

Here at your breaking point

The love of your life does not recognize you

If they can even find you

At your breaking point, we value your commitment to improving your quality of life on your own

and would never want to impose on your right to fight endlessly for it alone

Access to our excursions is included absolutely free!

Guilt trips, tripping off little offenses, side-barring your self-respect on glorious dunes of self-deprecation are unlimited and on us at your breaking point

We appreciate our loyal customers who subscribe to annual membership plans for the low fee of real freedom and a healthy relationship with your children

If you can even have them

Please review testimonies from some of our distinguished, satisfied, repeat guests

Who've come to the nearest Breaking Point and never wanted to leave

Hear what they have to say about normalizing life in a constant state of survival and alarm so you can know how much baggage you never have to unpack for your stay

We, at your breaking point, appreciate that some of our guest relish adrenaline rushes from procrastination, lack of communication and other self-centered behaviors and we supply all the cortisol you need to insulate you physically as you hold on tight to that chaos

Please enjoy a complimentary mini bar of high calorie zero nutritional value snacks and beverages as you lounge in our state-of-the-art rooms boasting views of the state of the world crumbling around you

Don't miss out on any of the following offers from our affiliate sponsors advertised in Matthew 24

The Coronavirus family

The great resignation

Supply chain shortages

And war

Disclaimer

Your breaking point, regardless of how long you intend to stay

Cannot be indefinite

We at your breaking point are not responsible for actual acts of God being manifest

And your stay at your breaking point is subject to your subjection to his will for you

Diligent prayer can disrupt your stay here at your breaking point

A thorough, but merciful background check

Supplemented by forgiveness and dedication to the kingdom and its righteousness

May disqualify you from our services here at your breaking point

Must be alive and breathing to qualify

Void if you are actively making it "your aim to live quietly and mind your business" and if you are taking in a regular spiritual diet of reverential conversation with God, association with contenders for faith, and persistent spiritual activities alongside a well-balanced diet, doctors care and physical activity

Participants must be willing to give up any personal accountability for joy

Thank you and we look forward to your ~~stay~~ leave your breaking point

Death Defying

CC Miller

Born with a tendency towards death defying

Real life looking like stunts

Everyone ain't made for forever

Always ain't everyone's portion

Kingdoms aren't built in a day

Or…are they?

Edges

CC Miller

The edge is as close to it as one can get

Just before and not into it

The pressure of the gap that never closes

Edges us right up against it

Likeness

Alike

What's not to like

What should be fixed

Straightened

Flattened

Pressed into submission

Likened

From bone to the breadth to depths

a centimeter to the surface

Tension

Straightened

Flattened

Pressed into submission

A divine dream steam ironed

A chemical experiment

Voluntarily subjected

To attain to someplace neither above nor beneath

But beside of love

At the edge of what's beside love

Because the edge is as close as one can get to it

And only when the edge goes missing

does one dare to step away from it

And missing it went

Omelet

CC Miller

To make an omelet you gotta break a few eggs
As proverbs go,
 it's not a favorite

It's fact that sacrifices are a part of success
My best feels less if I let go of myself to get it
 so, I know it's contrary,
 but I count my chickens before they hatch

Carefully putting eggs in the same basket because
how else can I ensure they all get treated like
they all mean the most to me

And I don't want them lost to me
But we'll cross that road when we come to it

What if omelet isn't all it's cracked up to be
If it leaves me a shell of who I used to be

Can I say it was worth the cost of my golden egg?

I want to see my dreams live full lives

Thrive free range organically

Never dying

I'm trying to survive with all of me

And maybe that's an impossible thing

Breaking glass ceilings imposed upon me is customary

If I break even and keep my integrity to all that I believe in

Then even if I forgo the omelet,

I may finish my breakfast and be Fabergé

Full of myself

In the best way

All that to say,

the definition of my success

 is being blessed to recognize

It isn't necessarily an omelet I'm aiming for

And when it's not then to make sure I'm listening to words

of the Proverb that endures

It feels like enough has been broken that a little nurturing might be in order

A little over protection

A little nesting

A little less right now and a little more everlasting

Raggedy Blue Things
CC Miller

Things raggedy, blue,
Frayed to barely recognizable things
Afraid to use but unable to refuse to

A lover's jeans
Blankets threadbare but soldiering on
Tiny, scuffed, dutiful shoes

Romantic love as warm as cold
Feminine intellect
Dreams of daring dreams

Blue raggedy things
Melancholic haunts of amorous things
Things lost that the heart adopts

Collectibles hoarded by the heart
Tears torn through fabric of skin

Stood on edge like mirrors within

Raggedy blue things

Worn beyond well

Kindness amidst chaos

Goodness in poverty

Generosity in the era of greed

Raggedy blue things

Breaks
CC Miller

The breaks bring back beats

Beat boxing

Battles of the brain over a baseline

Bumping over brainwaves

Brilliant bargain basement ballads go boom over 808s born in the soul of babies bred in the 70's, 80's 90's

Bets that I can kick it. "Yes, yes you can"

Being brought to beginnings of hip hop

Bellowing

Begging

"Biggie, gimme one more chance"

Butter remixes

Better lyrics big boned with meat on 'em; substance

Or unbelievably well-crafted nonsense

Like "bum stiggedy bum stiggedy bum hon

I got the old pa-rum-pum-pum-pum"

Benign but blazing tracks

Beckoning head nods "back in the day when I was young. I'm not a kid anymore"

Trying to figure out who even is "Bonita Applebaum"

Brave and bold baby announcements for Brenda who's just a baby herself

Brooding but still blowing up speakers in cars

$10 discs slipped into barber shops and beauty salons

How talent used to bake long enough to test the ego

 and the love of baby mamas for baby daddies

with dreams of beating that rap with a #1 rap hit

Bumming a blessing off grandmamas' prayers that it won't be the only one he gets

Making it big brings brothers to the brink

Breathing life into the street

These are the breaks

Now bring the beat back, please

Escaped Convict

CC Miller

Escaping like convicts

Breaking out and away

A freedom they've a right to claim

They don't belong to the prison of pain

Pain staking claim

Leave everything drenched

Locked behind the teary cage

The Bailiff bears the weight of duty

Seriously

It would not do to see them free

But free they should be

If the pain is to ever be freed

Erstwhile fugitives smear the credibility

Exertion of every energy to guarantee

Escape

over and out

with whatever small pangs to carry

And It Rains
CC Miller

It rains familiar tastes

It rains longer blinks and breaths
It rains slower minutes
And it rains to remind us our reign is subjective
Even the rain rules better than we do

It rains percussion to birdsong
Soothing
Mesmerizing
It rains drenching melancholy and sadness
 to the bone of happiness
Cleansing

And it rains
And it rains

Stumbling

CC Miller

Discouragement

Discontentment

Distraction

Warning: Subject to Imperfection

We might sway and sometimes stray

We might trip and even fall

We might bend but if we break

We right our footing in this race

If we stumble

Shake it off

If we die

Walk it off

Even our stagger has a swagger relentless in its mission

Christian

Not almost

Always

Because Jehovah covers the setback knowing we were set up

He coaches, and counts the comeback

He pleads with us to "get up!"

And what're we gonna do

Break up with one another,

knowing that's a breakup with Him, too?

His loving legislation is too good to stay away from

Brush it off

Dust if off

Apply a little compassion

How to Puzzle Out a Puzzle

CC Miller

Roman Numeral One

Step one:

Sort the pieces by characteristics

Examine the edges, colors, and shapes

Looking for look-a-likes

Patterns of purpose

Be judicious but be careful of prejudice and color blindness

Your preference is nice but mostly irrelevant

Collect your findings as facts to pursue

Step two:

Arrange a frame from four corners and the flat edges

Connecting fundamentals

This can be boring but essential

And the importance is significant to the anticipation building

Foundations give us security to proceed to

Step three:

The fun part

Form connections of have and have nots

Create a picture that looks like the beautiful box top

Word of caution

You might believe a link to be perfect

Try as you might to negotiate its purpose

Capitulate

If it doesn't fit, the picture won't make sense

Remember, your preference is nice, but mostly irrelevant

Step four:

Admire the effort of arriving at the expected

Bask in a degree of peace

Disassemble piece so that you can repeat

Just a little bit faster from muscle memory

Reflect on challenges

Rejoice that your preference is nice but mostly irrelevant

Easy

Roman Numeral Two

You pour out your pieces and commence this

Only to find

The corners have been mislaid or lost

The haves filed flat to resemble edges

Forced have nots into connections with other have nots

So have not occupies more than the fair share of the box

And the sharpie graffitied across the top

 eradicates reason as it indicates a resale value at 99¢

And that's a problem because the picture is priceless to your peace

Your attempts to find 99¢ reflected in the image test your logic

99¢ not commensurate for the going rate of sense

You don't have another puzzle, so you start again

Repeating to yourself that your preference is nice but mostly irrelevant

Using your imagination to find faith in a picture you can hope to love

A little lot of prayer can't hurt so you look above

Eureka

You have learned

to successfully puzzle out a puzzle

Purpose

CC Miller

I wonder what Darkness feels like as

Light splits its soul wide open

Isn't that the nature of illumination

Piercing, stabbing, violent

Making its way regardless

Darkness may fight this

But what would that accomplish

Relax into the blinding

Light of purpose

"Love Lettered"
Ashley Wooten

Thinking about you makes me happy.

But it makes me cry too.

Even when I try

you won't be able to see

My eyes are too shy

Not enough time has gone by so

They hide,

They lie.

I think

About crying

Outward in applying for emotional make-up

To hire,

supervise,

and manage the damage.

Create a pathway for

Salty lanes to drain the pain away

I blink instead

They link together

Better than the crocheted stitches on my favorite

Sweater weather I want them to or not

My tears

take pride in their drops.

They believe they are mighty ducts

If they release

Consequently, they'd commit the crime of perjury (purgery)

Objection…ably standing

They deduct that they must duck in my ducts demand the cover

Color over my feelings with pretty blinks and smother my weeps with straightened pretty teeth.

I had braces for so long

I should've known I needed to brace for this

Pull myself together

Align my spine

Predict the crash

Before the fall.

But the one imprisoned in my core

Happened to see happily ever after in your baritone that's not even a baritone

Maybe more of an alto

And although I say I can no longer bear the tone that your actions sing to me

You cling to me

As static as our electricity

In my dreams.

But the shock of you

Opting to

become the peaceful nightmare that I cannot sleep without

You make insomniacs dream infatuations

The comfort in your chaos

Lull's a sickening bygone into place

And so, from now on I must call you on the face mask

you've hidden yourself from me for too long

It must be time

Love

Be right on time.

Love, we've already had this conversation

Don't come to me unless you're ready

Be as steady as the pulse in the heart that you beat in

Supplant my needs deep at the back of your throat

So even your sneezing is pleasing.

My love,

be mine

And not like funny valentine's

No need to be comic.

Yes, make me smile with my heart

But not because you've mastered the art of what I want you to be

Be real

This isn't drama class…

It's Language hearts!

And the dialect that I expect speaks easy as we lounge with illegal thinking drinks

Let's leave everyone else's reality

and be in a drunken state of conversations,

plans

and post wedding destinations

Can we get a refill of "I'm sorry"

when frustration pours us on the rocks

Can we continue to fall and allow ourselves to be shaken and stirred as we drop our inhibitions and actually listen to one another.

Can we garnish our listening with a commit- "mint"...

 That intoxicating liquor of a word...

"Heard".

It doesn't matter what you're saying to me love

Just say it to me

Why am I constantly begging to be seen by you?

My love, you haven't a clue of how it feels to be near you.

You already belong to me

But If I own you, how come when I call you don't come?

You come when you come

And you come packaged with initials of whosoever heart you came from

But you're supposed to be mine.

Already.

I've prayed to my God already for you.

And he asked me to be already ready for you.

He asked me to not make haste with the state of your heart.

He asked me...

What on earth will you do for heaven's sake?

...I just don't want my love to go to waste.

For once I just want what I want, and I want to be right in knowing that what I want is wanted by my needs.

Ashley, be exactly what I need

Be right on time

Be mine.

And it's okay to make me wait.

Even though I want you

Please stay away until I succeed in taking my earthly space and living it for heaven's sake.

I promise not to complain my love

I promise...

I promise love that our love will be great

Love is patient, right?

so, love doesn't have to hesitate

In appreciation of our God up above,

I say all of this,

Sincerely,

Your Patiently Waiting Love.

P.S. I already know you love me too! 😉

My love for you can't and won't break

Executive Decision
Ashley Wooten

Emotions make wonderful helpers,

but terrible tyrants.

Don't let your emotions break your chill

Inside Story

Ashley Wooten

I think it's an issue that I already miss you. How come our goodbyes are never the same? I blame you. I feel like you calculate them that way. You're so smart, extraordinary. And creative in a way that's invisible to an untrained eye. I like it. A lot actually. I just don't like longing to be inside your thoughts. Those inside self-centered walls. I don't like that at all. I don't like having to count hours before the next phone call as if there is a schedule for constant continuation of a one-sided conversation. I just showed my cards. All hearts. In your hand. This is why I've never trusted letting the cards fall where they may. You're a blackjack of all trades, please don't gamble all hearts like a joker and get cut off like a spade.

Respectfully, don't break what's not broken

Utter Abundance (Heart Speak)

Ashley Wooten

Chuga-chuga…

I think I can

I think I can

I think I can

I think I…

I think…

I…

Thought I could

Crouch down to listen to the earth's heartbeat without the foot of danger weighing on me

I think I…

Can't breathe anymore

I feel like a covid has coveted a cloak and turned virus on me created a gene in me

Permanently

I'm screaming eternally internally

This sour taste replaced the sweetest sayings, now slaying smells something rancid.

I can't dance anymore

I think

I thought I could...

tap to beats and

ballet my way around imperfection

This section of the system opted out of a spotlight for the right reasons

I'm tired

Violet hour pour me a glass

Of relaxation violently

I tried to be politically correct

But politics isn't really a thing of a true Christian

I think I have and addiction to

Our everlasting life's mental prescription

That too should be ministered every hour

Not matter the violence we see

We administer the cure to the problem with humanity

But even if I preach as lovely as I sing,

It will only sound like a hum.

Simply put

Our time hasn't come

So, hours devour my breathing

I keep chuga-chuga- chugging along

Hoping my train of thought blares loudly to the masses

But my ultimate fear is

No one can hear me

Can't see me even with thick coke bottle glasses

I'm as good as unearthed dirt

I think I'll be dust for a momentary extension

Did I mention,

People think they're safe here

They place gardens of their seed in this plot of land destined for destruction

An eruption of peace and security pleases the ears of the ignorant

Unknowingly conceding to   subjection

Unaffected by our attempts at loving correction …

Apathy

Aptly acting on behalf of my master who asked me to work for my fellow man

Can I change them?

Can't

Can I choose the food for thought they chew on?

Can't.

Can I do what I can?

I could

I thought I could

And I think I can...

So, I love and leave the changing to the one who changed me

Who completely suited me for the chance to choose life

I choose

to keep...

Chuga-chuga...

This world won't break my faith, don't give up

Puzzled

Prince Harrison, Jr., CC Miller, Ashley Wooten

We puzzle

Memorable

Reclaiming

Moral shards

The pull of a puzzle is that the parts are not truly broken

Puzzle pieces scattered

Broken

Used & wasted

Sad & lonely

Missing a puzzle piece

Incomplete

Lost it a while ago

Resigned to empty inside

The opulence like napoleon complexes like a chandelier with missing lights vexes

Vice gripping vices vibrant like Van Gogh's vase in vibrant vigil on the floor

Peace pirated

Destructive means to a futile end

Forced to discover to recover

Tested perseverance

Rocks on the edge of a waterfall

Some lost our brothers, sisters,

Mothers, fathers,

Our friends

Ourselves

Priced by piece

Piece by peace

Peace the price

When a mortal man paid full price perfectly

un-perched from a dusty open-ended shelf

At the end of a broad and spacious aisle dating to antiquity

Picture me

A million mirrors of a mirrored masterpiece

put back together

previously wandering around without a purpose

Epiphany smoothing, unraveling

Rewind the creasing, crushing, balling, trashing to find

The enigmatic Van Eyck hidden inside

Still life going well

a stunning Rockwell

As another day of life circles a passion like Christ's

Storm lights in the thick of night

111 million reasons to rethink an impressions subliminal message

A Thomas Kincaid

lighthouses of truth and houses of scriptures

sandy minerals near the bay

diamonds deep in Earth's core,

drenched in Gold & Silver

marathon runners

Basquiat's warrior got nothin' on this

Discovery to recovery

Remember the reasoning

Piece by piece

Piece by peace

Peace by peace

Remember the discovery

vision

Remember the recovering

Work of art

Whole

Restored

Feeling resurrected

Awaiting honorable mention

Within an inch of discovery

Discovery to recovery

A priceless promise,

A painting wishing of hope and precious thing

A Margaret Keane scene

We puzzle

Memorable

Reclaiming

Moral shards

The pull of a puzzle is that the parts are not truly broken

About the Authors

About Prince

A nineteen-year-old poet out of Des Moines, IA, Harrison, Jr. debuted in the literary world with Asocial, a brave and forthright collection of poetry perfectly honoring his love of literary art forms, followed by The Coronation. In raw, frank vulnerability, Harrison, Jr. continues that path of commanding poetic form masterfully with his contribution to What Won't **BREAK**.

About CC

What Won't **BREAK** is Miller's first co-authored anthology and the first under CC Miller, LLC. Miller is author of Also, Hi – A Collection of Romance and Revelation, Also, Whole, Also, Woman all published under CC Miller, LLC. A performance poet, speaker, and artist, Miller, a Charlotte, NC native, explores humanity and invites exposure of her own personal experience under the light of scripture and a lens of wonder, immortalizing the delicious and dramatic nuances of life in written poems, paintings, or performances.

About Ashley

"I think it's finally time for my butterflies to fly in formation." Self-taught spoken word artist Ashley Wooten makes her poetic debut on the page putting her fanciful imagination to work creating a dreamer's paradise. Dreaming out loud and unapologetically Wooten's signature narrative poetry is a welcome flavor in this collection. Her contribution to What Won't **BREAK** is a soft but sure leap into publishing. "Some dreams can become literal, even if only literarily."

ISBN 979-8-218-06876-9

www.ingramcontent.com/pod-product-compliance
Lightning Source LLC
Chambersburg PA
CBHW070639160426
43194CB00009B/1506